Wow!

If you are reading this thank you for helping me live out my dream. Over the years that I have been writing I never would have imagined that I would make it this far. I would like to thank the following: My sister Chanelle my first audience member, my mother Linda my biggest cheerleader, my baby sister Ronelle, Maurice, my nieces Janea, Ciera and Anaiya, my nephew Jakhi, my big cousins Lisa, Karen, Barbara, China, Chakell, Charelle, Shontae, Sqeekey, Cliffton and all their offspring, my favorite Aunt Cheryl, Grandma Dora, Aunt Muffin, my extended family Nadine, Aunt Nellie, Gail, Edie, Melinda, Torrey, Genelle, Teddy, Brianna to my homegirls, Rhoda, Adrian, Nik and Talisa.

To Mr. & Mrs. Etheridge, Sheila, Derek, Dee Dee, Desi, Danielle, Danielle S, Yakini, Chase, their family and the Flushing crew. To my SR.com web family who gets me through my workday, to Kesha thanks for the art work, to Cherise at Perks, to Mike from Hue-man book store. Thank you all.

I want to send a special thank you to the two special men in my life. My baby Jaylen, who keeps me on my toes. I love you so much and your voice will never be silenced. I can't wait for the day that the world will hear you. You truly are a gift from God. To my better half Bill. If it wasn't for you this book would still be sitting on my hard drive. I want to thank you for pushing me, believing in me, advocating for me and being there day and night helping me shape what has now become my first published novel. I know what this was and I know that because of your support; what it has become.

RIP to my father Leroy Huggins, & Michael Jackson

I GOTTA MAKE IT TO HEAVEN FOR GOING THRU HELL

A NOVEL BY IESHA WOMACK

Part One:

Going Through

As the sun began its descent on another 90 plus degree day in NYC, Summer was winding down her day at her salon, Heaven. During a typical week she wouldn't have had as many customers, but with it being the weekend before the fourth of July, her salon was more crowded than usual. Even though she loved the additional business, today was a day she really wanted, almost needed to be home. She was considering leaving early, but between appointments and walk-ins, the closer it got to closing time the more customers filled the chairs.

"Summer did you see where I put my purse?" Her thoughts were interrupted by Constance, a close friend as well as one of her beauticians.

"No" If she only kept up with her things like she did that man she dated she would be better off, Summer thought to herself.

"Damn. I had it when I went to lunch."

"I don't know Constance, maybe you left it in the restaurant."

"Who said I went to a restaurant for lunch?"

"Girl you know you are too much." Renee chimed in from her chair as she got her hair rolled by one of the assistants.

"You know me girl, I'd rather be paid to put things in my mouth for lunch than to pay to put things in my mouth." Constance said slapping Renee a high five.

"I hear that girl." Renee said "That's exactly why this dude I was seeing got cut the fuck off. He was talking about he made $30,000 a year teaching kids. I mean I love the kids but that shit ain't enough to take me to dinner."

Summer had become so sick of them with their immature gold digging ways. It seemed as if it never stopped.

"Renee, don't you make enough money at the phone company? What is it you need a man to do that you can't do yourself?"

Renee looked at her with a perplexed look. "Fuck me, that's what."

Summer didn't even respond. She just continued to add the perm to her customer's hair.

"Besides that Summer," Constance intervened. "Aren't you the one who introduced her to that dude anyway?"

Here she goes again with her simple mentality Summer thought to herself. "Yes I did, because he was my friend and a nice guy, not because I reviewed his job application." She said rolling her eyes. She was trying to do Renee a favor as she was going through her drama with her boyfriend at the time.

"Summer, you know me. You should know better than to try and set me up with a dude with no *paper*." Renee said accentuating the word "paper" in a high pitched tone while checking her nails to make sure they still looked immaculate. "Then to top it off the fool..."

"Would you please call him by his name? Thomas, not fool." Summer stated, clearly annoyed.

"Well excuse the hell out of me." Renee said, laughing along with Constance and half the shop.

"You need to stop focusing on what's in a man's pockets." Summer said, still trying to defend her friend.

"I would have to agree with her there Ree, it's not what's in his pockets but what's in his pants that counts." This time the whole shop within listening range broke out in laughter agreeing. The ringing of the phone saved Summer the headache of responding to Constance and her immature comment.

"Good evening Heaven, How may I help you?"

"Hey." It was her husband David.

"Hi" He was the last person she wanted to hear from right now.

"You still upset?"

"Why would you call me and ask me something like that David?"

"Because I want to know, that's why? You barely said two words to me this morning."

"Well I damn sure am not going to talk about this over the phone."

"Pumpkin, you know I still love you."

"Really?" She said rhetorically.

"Of course I do." He answered obviously not catching the hint.

"I'll speak to you when I get home in case you haven't noticed I'm at work."

"What time will you be home?"

"I don't know."

"Summer, we really need to talk." Although she sensed and appreciated the urgency and concern in his voice, she didn't have time to address it.

"I'm in the middle of something; I'll speak to you when I get home." She said before abruptly hanging up.

Summer couldn't believe that he had the nerve to call her and act like nothing happened. He acted as if he hadn't said the things he said the night before. He was the reason that she was letting Constance and Renee get to her the way they were today. Any other time she would just brush them off, but today her nerves were frazzled.

Last night she called and informed David that it was that time of the month which meant she was ovulating and needed him to be home early. He walked through the door at 12:59 am. He tried to quietly slip into the shower downstairs and then ease himself into the bed. She couldn't believe he had the nerve to get into bed and not even acknowledge the fact that it was after 1 am.

"Where have you been all night?" Was the first thing she said in a monotone voice.

"I didn't mean to wake you Pumpkin."

"Well you did. Now, where were you?" She replied this time her voice tinged with anger.

"I had to work late. Where do you think I was?"

"I called you at 3:00 and told you I needed you home early."

"Well I couldn't make it. How in the hell do you think you can call me two hours before it's time to get off, talking about you need me home early. I do work too."

"It's one in the morning." She said almost screaming.

"Exactly."

"Exactly. So where the hell have you been, because I called your office and they said you left a little after 6." This time she did scream

"So what is it? You keeping tabs on me now?" He yelled back

"Don't try and change the subject on me tonight. You knew how important tonight was for me and you missed it." She said while choking back tears.

"Summer please, how many times are we going to go through this? Why can't we just adopt?"

"Is that what you want David?"

"I just want this shit to be over with. I'm tired of trying."

"I can't believe you're saying this knowing this is something I want more than anything."

"Look Summer, I can't continue to carry on like this. It's either we're going to get pregnant the way most people do or we won't."

"Dave, you know better than anybody that I would love to just get pregnant the way most people do, but I can't. Which still doesn't explain where the hell you've been all night." The tears had begun to slowly make their way down her face.

"Clearing my mind that's where. Did you ever stop to think if *I* want to keep going through this torture just to have a baby?" That last comment made her sit up.

"I didn't know it was 'torture' for you." Her anger immediately stopped the tears from falling any longer.

"Can we just please go to sleep?"

"No David, we can't. You know how much I want a baby and if you don't feel the same this is not something we should go to sleep on."

"Maybe not, but I am." That was the last words exchanged between them until his call today.

"Summer." Renee said interrupting her thoughts from the prior evening.

"What?" She said looking at Renee.

"Do you think I need to get a filling?" She asked raising her hand in Summer's face.

"No, they look fine." She told her in a disinterested tone.

"I told you Constance." Renee said rolling her eyes at Constance.

"You listen to her if you want to." Constance said, a bit perplexed by Summer's dismissive attitude. She knew fully well that Summer should be encouraging as much business as she could as opposed to turning some down. "When was the last time you got those nails done?'

"Two weeks ago." Renee said looking at them again contemplating if she should in fact get them refilled.

"I hate to be the one to tell you this, but it looks like three weeks ago." Constance said while finishing up her customer's hair, spraying some hair sheen. "Close your eyes baby."

"Summmmer." Renee whined her name which really annoyed Summer.

Even though she knew Renee practically all her life she still couldn't get use to her spoiled ways. She had met Renee back in the seventh grade when all the other girls hated Renee because of the same reasons that annoyed her to this day. She was an only child who was used to getting any and everything she wanted. Her parents did everything they could to provide the best for her. Summer could still remember the way the jealous girls use to tease and pick on Renee because she always had the latest and best of everything. It was during the end of their school year that she befriended Renee, after hearing of a plot of some girls planning to jump and rob Renee after school. It was on that hot June day that Summer defended Renee and automatically became her best friend whether she wanted to or not.

"Renee do you think you need to have your nails done over?"

"I don't know. That's what I have you for. Don't you know you're responsible for my beauty?"

"Aren't you going out this weekend?" Constance butted in.

"You're right Connie, maybe I should leave you in charge of my beauty."

Renee said giving Summer a what's up with you look. "Terri, how many people do you have?" She said to the manicurist.

"Just two." Terri replied.

"Well make sure I'm next." Renee said

After Summer finished perming her customer's hair, she sent her over to the hair wash station, took another girl from under the dryer and started to blow out her hair. The phone rang again and she answered it hoping it wasn't her husband again.

"Good evening Heaven."

"Hi God ma it's me, is my mom still there?"

"Hey baby, she sure is, hold on." She handed the phone to Constance.

"Hello."

"Mama, Granny said what time are you coming to get me?"

"When I'm done, why what's the problem?"

"I'm tired."

"Then take your ass to sleep. I'll be there when I'm done and not before."

She could hear her daughter repeating what she said to her grandmother.

"Granny said for you to hurry up because she got Bingo tonight."

"Whatever, I'll see you when I get there."

Hearing Constance talk to her daughter Meagan that way always hurt Summer to her heart. Here she was trying any and everything to have a chance at motherhood and Constance, blessed with such a beautiful and smart daughter acted as if she would rather do without her. She even acted as if Meagan was a hindrance. Constance's primary focus in life was that married man she was sleeping with. Summer could bet her life that despite her mother's pleas Constance would make time for a pit stop to meet him before she went home. It was as if Renee was reading her mind because the next words out of her mouth were. "Connie, you going to see Reggie tonight?"

"No girl I met him for lunch today."

"Did you speak to him about what we spoke about?"

"What, about him leaving his wife? No."

"Why not? I thought we agreed you would talk to him."

"I will… when the time is right."

"Connie you've been seeing this man for two years, now *is* the time."

"Renee you don't know enough about our relationship to say that."

"I know enough..."

"Renee, sit under this dryer I'm about to take Honey from under and Constance you take off the rest of the night and go pick up your child."

"Take off? Summer you still have three people under the dryer."

"No, I have two people under the dryer because I'm taking Honey out now. Then I have Nancy and Renee and she don't even count. You go and pick my baby up and take her home."

"You sure?"

"If I wasn't sure would I suggest it?"

"Okay then, call me when you get home." She gathered her things, said goodnight and left. Not two minutes after she was gone Renee started in about her. "I can't believe she still hasn't ended it with his ass. I told her she needs to end it before she gets so involved she *can't* leave."

Right now all Summer wanted to do was finish up, close the shop and go home. She was not in the mood to engage in everybody's gossip. Before anyone could ask her opinion, Honey the customer whose hair she was currently styling chirped in. "You can't stop that girl from seeing that man, she's already in too deep. Connie loves him Renee, you need to accept that." Summer hated when Renee spoke about Constance with others when she wasn't around. It was okay for her to speak about her when it was just the two of them but discussing it with Honey was a bit much. Honey was a local stripper who always wanted wild and exotic hair styles to make her stand out amongst the other dancers. Summer, being well known for her exotic hair styles she was able to satisfy Honey's taste and she became an instant regular. Summer even used Honey as a hair model in hair shows that she did throughout the country. Although Honey was a regular customer Summer *never* viewed her as one of the girls. She sure as hell didn't understand where Renee got off discussing Constance with her.

"Accept it, Are you crazy? As long as I call her my girl I will never accept it. Right Summer?" She asked expecting Summer to agree.

"Renee you just need to worry about who you're sleeping with."

"Everybody." Honey said laughing

"Excuse me, I think not King magazine hoe of the month."

"And proud of it too Miss October." Honey said laughing and bouncing her fake boobs at the same time. "You want a peek."

"No." Renee said now turned off from Honey and the whole exchange. Summer was relieved because she shut up, opened a book and started to read. Finally a little peace and quiet or so she thought until Honey started talking again.

"Summer I was reading in the paper. They were talking about the big hair show in Texas this weekend, you going?"

"No, not this year." Summer said

"Why not? I was wondering why you haven't spoken on it. I thought you were trying to leave me out this year." Honey said watching her intently through the mirror. The whole shop was covered with mirrors and the theme was blue and white resembling the sky and clouds.

She had named the shop after her daughter who died 2 weeks and three days after being born of SIDS. After the loss of the baby, Summer went into a deep depression for the next year and a half. Her husband was extremely influential in her opening the shop to try and help her cope with their loss. Even though he always referred to it as their loss she always believed he viewed it as *her* loss. After losing Heaven she had quit her job and consumed herself with trying to get pregnant again. It had happened twice for her but each time she lost the child. The first she lost at four months, while the second she lost the day after she discovered she was pregnant. Opening the shop was something that helped keep her from consuming herself with getting pregnant, which was just what her husband wanted and she needed. Despite the business being extremely successful she was back at it again. After seeing all the young girls come in to get their hair done for Easter and Graduation or the ones who wanted her to "hook them up." For their baby shower, Summer once again wanted a baby more than anything… and she was willing to do anything to get it.

...Constance

Driving down the highway, all Constance could do was think about getting to Reggie. She had called him as soon as Summer told her she could leave for the day. Her mother wasn't going to any Bingo game, she just wanted her to rush home and get Meagan. Besides that, even if she was going, she wasn't going right this minute. Reggie would often lie to his wife just to get out for a few hours to be with her. She loved him so much and couldn't understand why he wouldn't leave his "fat ass" wife. Following his wife on numerous occasions in an effort to catch her cheating had proved worthless. Constance even carried a camera at all times, not to catch the memorable moments of her daughter's childhood but just in case she ever ran into his wife doing something she shouldn't. She dreamed of Reggie receiving a package at his office with photos of Patty and some unidentified man engaged in passionate poses. This would be the straw that would have him filing for divorce and running back to her arms to be with her. This type of thinking made perfect sense to her.

As she pulled into the hotel parking lot, she looked for Reggie's car, which she did not see. This annoyed her because Reggie chose this particular place because it was close to his house, but of course not too close. This way he could say he was going to the store and be back in enough time such that nothing was out of the ordinary. She hated the fact that he treated her like a "drive thru" as Renee liked to put it. 'Girl you are like a ATM or fast food drive thru for that man, pussy on the go.' As she sat in the lot Renee's voice echoed through her head and deep inside she knew Renee was right. After she checked into the hotel she called her mother and told her she would be there in an hour. She estimated Reggie getting there in the next fifteen minutes, which meant she would be out of there in the next half hour. It would take her another forty five minutes to drive across town to get to her house. While this was more than the estimated time she told her mother, she didn't care, since her focus was to see Reggie once more before she went home. Her phone started to ring in her bag and from the ring tone playing she knew it was Reggie.

"Hello."

"Hey, don't be mad." Was the first thing Reggie said as her heart sank preparing for the blow he was about to hit her with.

"Where are you Reggie?" she said optimistically hoping he would say he was outside the door, but like many times before reality tapped her on the shoulder and reminded her this was Reggie we were talking about.

"I'm in the bathroom. Don't you hear the water running? She thinks I'm in the shower." He whispered into his cell phone.

"Why haven't you left yet Reggie? I called you forty five minutes ago. I'm already at the hotel." She wanted to cry. She couldn't believe she drove thirty minutes out of her way just to be stood up. The shop was only five minutes from her house and 15 minutes away from her mother's house. Now she had to drive forty five minutes back to her mother's house both hurt and sexually frustrated.

"Well I'm sorry. I'll give you the money back tomorrow when I pick you up. We'll make up tomorrow, okay?" How could she stay mad at him, he was so apologetic.

"What happened? I thought you said you were going to tell her you were going to run to the store?"

"I did except I didn't expect her to tell me she picked up what I was going to get." Constance wanted to be mad but she couldn't. She knew the best thing for her to do was get in her car and go home to get her baby. She always felt guilty about leaving Meagan but never guilty enough to stop her routine. Meagan's father was a low life who could be considered her high school sweetheart except there was nothing sweet about him. He terrorized everybody Constance loved. She loved and hated him for that same reason; she loved the strength in him but despised his controlling behavior. With her own father leaving her mother when she was just five years old, she always longed for someone to protect her. Matthew having the entire school terrified of him made him perfect for her. The biggest downfall was he also abused her. Three weeks after her 19th birthday Matthew got arrested and two weeks after that she found out she was two months pregnant. Thinking that the baby would fill the void left by the man in her life she opted to keep the baby against her mother's will. Her mother begged her to go to

college and forget about Matthew. Although she had moved on without him she never forgot about Matthew. He was now serving his eighth of a 15 year sentence. It would be a long time before he saw the light of day so Constance regularly sent him pictures of Meagan during her birthday and holidays. She never led him on to think she would wait for him. She wanted him to know that his daughter was well and he always respected her for that.

"You owe me big time for this one." She said to Reggie while flopping down on the bed.

"Look I just saw you this afternoon then you call me at the last minute and I owe you because I wasn't able to get out, please. I said I tried. It's not my fault she went shopping before she came home." She could hear the irritation building in his voice so she quickly changed the subject before he became too upset.

"I was laying here in my red teddy, the one that hugs my tits just the way you like it." She said trying to initiate some phone sex out of him. She was so horny and she did already pay for the room.

"Are you touching yourself?"

"You know I am."

"Where do you have your hand at?"

"In my pussy."

"Excuse me."

"I mean in your pussy." She knew it drove him wild when she didn't refer to her pussy as his pussy the same way it drove her crazy knowing he was in the bathroom having phone sex while his wife was downstairs probably preparing dinner. *"Is it hot and wet the way I like it?"*

"Aaahhhhh baby it's so hot and wet."

"I wanna hear it." She took the phone and put it next to her pussy so he could hear her sticking her fingers in and out. At this time he took his manhood out and started to stroke it with measured, slow motions.

"Did you hear it baby?"

"Yeah I heard it. Now I want to cum all in that pussy. Do you want me to stick this big hard dick in that pussy?"

"Yes." She moaned. *"I wanna taste that big dick in my mouth."*

"Aaah baby that sounds so good."

"You feel me sucking it? I love sucking that dick. Can you tell how much I love sucking that big black beautiful dick?"

"Stick your finger in your ass for me. Are you doing it baby?"

"Yes, I want you to taste me baby I'm about to cum please taste me." He didn't respond. She stopped what she was doing and listened closely. She could hear him saying something but wasn't sure what it was because the voices were coming out mumbled like he had the phone under something. Shortly following the mumbling her ear was met with the dial tone. She waited at the hotel for another thirty minutes hoping he would call back but he didn't.

When she got to her mother's house to pick Meagan up she was already asleep. This was the third time this week she had picked her up while she was asleep. She felt bad knowing once she woke her up they would be rushing to get her off to school and she wouldn't see her again until tomorrow evening when she got home from work. She hoped it wouldn't be so crowded at the shop tomorrow so she could get out of there early and spend a little time with Meagan. However, with tomorrow being the Saturday before the fourth of July which fell on Sunday this year she knew the place would be packed. Her appointment book alone was booked until eight O'clock not to mention what ever walk ins they may take. She was hoping that Summer would turn walk ins away tomorrow since they were already booked with appointments.

She and Summer had been friends for as long as she could remember living. Their mothers were best friends and raised them as sisters. When Summer's mother died three years ago it hurt Constance just as much if not more than Summer. Constance, who was named after Summer's mother, had a close connection with her and she still pained over her death. She could still remember how they would always spend the night at each others house as children and even now as adults. They always either lived in the same building or within walking distance of each other. Even now Summer only lived twenty minutes away from her by car. Summer now lived in Bayside, Queens where she owned a three bedroom house with her husband David.

When Summer first met and married David 6 years ago she was so happy for her. David was as close to perfect as perfect could get back then, but lately she wondered about them as a couple. David had changed within the past few years especially in the past few months. In Constance's opinion he was showing signs of a cheating husband. Signs she knew too well because the man she was cheating with had told many of the same lies to his wife that she would hear David often say to Summer. Of course she never discussed any of this with Summer, because as much as she loved Summer all the girl cared about was having a baby and nothing was going to get in her way.

As she reached her two bedroom apartment the first thing she saw was her cat Miffy, who ran over to her purring and rubbing her body over Constance's legs before she shooed her away.

She put Meagan in her bed and on her way out she noticed a picture her daughter had left on her night stand. The picture was of a family, with the father drawn far away from the mommy and the daughter. She felt bad that her daughter had to grow up without a father just like she had. She only wished she could somehow help make up for what her father was unable to provide. The ringing of her cell phone startled her.

"Hello."

"I'm sorry."

"Reggie?"

"I'm on my way over to your house right now."

"What? And what about Patty?"

"Since when did you start worrying about Patty?"

"Reggie, you just told me you couldn't get out, now you're on your way over here?"

"Patty's on the rag. I'm on my way over there now." And he hung up before she could say another word. Not having too much time, she started to straighten up her apartment. It wasn't much but it was hers as long as she could continue to pay the rent. It wasn't as nice as Summer's where custom made furniture filled the living room and they entertained company in the "family" room as they so eloquently put it. She always wanted to ask them "what family?" Ain't no damn kids running around here because if they were, trust me you wouldn't have this expensive ass furniture in your living room. Knowing that was a sour spot with Summer she never dared mentioned her feelings on the matter. She did however find out that the expensive 'museum room' as Renee called it, was all David's idea. She knew her girl couldn't be so pompous as to have living room furniture worth five figures just because it was once owned by Sammy Davis Jr. That was more David's style. Her downstairs buzzer went off. "Who is it?" "It's me, open the door." She buzzed him in running to the mirror to double check her hair and make up. She always wanted him to see her looking her best. Fortunately working at the shop she was able to at least keep her hair and nails done. Tonight she was sporting a doobie wrap, her dyed black hair always shined and smelled as if she had just got it done, her weave was tight. It looked very much like one of those actresses or video dancers on television. This made sense given that Summer had put in many of those same actresses and dancers weaves in at the shop.

Growing up Constance had been teased because of her dark skin. She was called everything from midnight to boogie man. It was her aunt Connie who helped her embrace her dark skin. Her aunt was also dark skinned and had known what Constance felt. The family support that Connie gave to her niece was the biggest bond the two shared with each other. Summer being conceived by a Puerto Rican father didn't have that problem as her light skin separated her from big Connie and Constance.

Now tonight 20 years later here she was with a paid, fine ass black man. Even though he was married, in Constance's heart she felt he was hers. DING DONG. She opened the door praying her daughter didn't hear.

"What are you doing here?" she asked him taking the grocery bags out of his hands that he was carrying.

"Is that your way of asking me to leave? See I even think about you when I'm shopping." He said while grabbing her into a bear hug feeling on her behind.

"I thought that was it for tonight."

"Yeah, well that's your problem you think too much. You need to do more undressing and less talking. I don't have all night to be here you know."

"Yeah I know." I don't know why he's yelling he's the one who decided to come over, Constance thought to herself.

"Well then act like it and come here." He grabbed her in his arms and started to kiss her.

"Let's go in the room, I don't want my daughter to wake up and catch us out here."

"That's more like it." He said while slapping her rear on the way to the bedroom.

...Renee

As Renee drove around her parking garage looking for a spot she thought about calling somebody over for a night cap but was too tired and quickly killed the thought. Today had been a long day for Renee. She hadn't even told Summer about what happened and she told Summer *everything.* When she woke up this morning she never would've thought she'd be sleeping alone tonight. None of her friends knew that for the past six months her on again off again fiancé Frog had been staying with her again. He obtained the nick name Frog because when he dunked a basketball it was as if he leaped like a frog. Renee and Sean (aka Frog) had been going through their thing for the past 4 years. Two years ago as a seemingly first step towards marriage he bought her an engagement ring. Two years later, he still wouldn't commit to a wedding date. Renee decided she wouldn't commit either, so she often stepped outside of the relationship.

She refused to sit around and wait for him to make up his mind to marry her. She knew it was her fault for allowing him to taste the milk before buying the cow. She felt he was starting to make her look like a fool and there was no way she was going to be strung along for another year without setting a date. Last night she had planned an elaborate candlelight dinner. She wore a black off the shoulder mini Fendi dress with a pair of strappy Manolo Blahnik shoes he had bought her for Valentines Day. When Frog first entered the apartment he didn't know what was going on but he soon got the picture and became excited when he saw Renee sitting under that candle light with that black dress on. "It smells good in here."

"Is that all you have to say to me?" She said getting up from the table revealing her long sexy legs. Standing at 5'9" Renee's legs looked stunning in the short dress and heels.

"Well, you look and smell good too. I'm not sure what's going on, but I'm thinking I'm a little underdressed for the occasion." He said tugging at his oversized white t-shirt. He had on a pair of blue shorts and blue and white Nikes. His scent was an African oil she had specially made for him at the Nubian Heritage Boutique in Harlem. He never cared much for fragrances and grooming products aside from a doo rag but he knew that she loved doing stuff like that for him so he didn't mind wearing it. Besides that, he loved the scent and on numerous occasions females of all ages would ask him what he was wearing that smelled so good. Frog could only respond that he didn't know and always proudly stated. "My girl picked it out for me." He knew this was another reason she went and spent $50.00 for the little 10fl oz bottle every month and never told him what it was or where it came from. She just made sure he always had some on hand. This was how Renee was with him. She loved him and now she wondered if she had lost that love forever.

She had prepared tonight's evening in hopes that he would finally commit to a wedding date. She already reneged on a promise to herself by shacking up with him long term without him deciding on a date. She had even been completely faithful since he started staying with her which was a slight change in her routine.

"What's going on? Are you pregnant or something?" *Why does he always think I'm trying to trap him with a baby?* "No Sean, I'm not pregnant. I just wanted to try and do something nice for us."

"Baby I know you, you're up to something. If you wanna play, fine I'll play. I'm hungry. What did you make?"

"I made short ribs with rice and vegetables, so sit down so we can eat." After they finished dinner they were laying around on the couch listening to some Marvin Gaye. Renee now full and tired began to doze off when she started to feel him rubbing on her breast. "Sean."

"Yeah."

"You know I love you right?"

"I love you too baby. Let's go get in the bed."

"We need to talk."

"Here we go, I knew this was for something." He said while sitting up on the couch.

"I was thinking and I think it's time we set a date for the wedding."

"And who's going to pay for this wedding? You know you have expensive taste, Nah baby not now. Now is not the time."

"It's either now or never. I've walked around for 2 years with this ring on my finger without a date. If you weren't ready to marry me, why the hell would you buy me a ring?"

"I'm not getting into this with you tonight. I have enough stress at work. I don't need to come in here and have to deal with your shit too."

She couldn't believe he was sitting here talking to her like this. Had he lost his mind, she almost slapped him but thought better of it.

"Sean, I know you're not going to sit here and talk to me like this. And to have the nerve to say us setting a wedding date is 'my shit'. Excuse me but I thought you proposed to me."

"Babe, all I'm saying is today is not the day for this. I come in here, see you looking and smelling all good with the place all lit up with candles. That was nice but to know you only did this to bring up this wedding shit is crazy. If that was the case you should've just said that when I first walked in the door. Don't wait until a nigga is full and horny to run game on me. You know better than that."

"Sean I've been walking around with this ring for two years with no date in sight. If you're not serious about marrying me, you need to let me know now."

"Set a date then." He said looking her in her eyes, conceding to the moment.

"Are you serious?" she knew he was serious. He would've never joked with her about something like that. He would get his shit and leave before he joked about something like that.

"Don't ask me am I serious. Set a date, you went through all of this to get a date, so set it."

"I don't know." She hadn't expected for him to give in so easily. She anticipated going back and forth in a war over when they would get married. She never thought it would be this easy. His quick concession surprised her. Any other time he would flat out say "Not now" or he would just change the subject but not this time. She had to think fast before he changed his mind.

"How about next summer? This gives us time to plan something nice… lets say July 18th." He just sat looking at her with a silly smile on his face exposing his chip tooth that she always found so sexy on him. Sean stood 6'4" and had a medium build. His caramel skin was flawless for a man and his light brown eyes sparkled with his smile. Sitting there watching him watch her like that only turned her on. The fact that he finally committed to a wedding date didn't hurt either.

"You're crazy, you know that?" He finally said. "Where the hell did you get the 18th from? How do you even know it's on a weekend? You had this all planned down to the day." All Renee could do was laugh because he was right. She did have the 18th set in the back of her mind. Getting married was something she wanted more than anything so she did have her plan all laid out but couldn't let him know that. "I did not." She said wrapping her arms around him and kissing him. When they made love that night it was with more love and compassion than the two of them had ever shared. She was finally able to let her walls down because she felt that he finally let his down.

When Renee went to work the next morning, she floated on cloud nine. Her morning was going by like a breeze. Her boss, who she had slept with a few times during her most frustrating times with Sean walked into her office and closed the door. She knew it would be trouble.

"Good afternoon."

Even though she abstained from giving it up to him in the past few months as her and Sean were working things out she did fool around with him every so often; letting him feel her up, playful flirting or a lunch date here or there. She didn't know why she kept this up with him when her and Sean were doing so well since they had gotten back together.

"How are you this afternoon Raymond?" she said with a pencil in her mouth being as sexy as she always was.

"Thinking about you. I saw you come in here today with that nice red outfit on and I just thought I'd drop in to tell you how sexy you looked." She did look good and she also felt great today. She sported a red Donna Karan New York blazer with matching mini skirt that she had fitted to hug her in all the right places. Fortunately she had maintained her figure over the last year.

"Well thank you for noticing, but I have a lot of work to catch up on."

"I sent your assistant on an errand." Raymond mentioned matter of factly.

"And" Renee said almost laughing because she knew what he was getting at.

"And" Raymond said walking over to her. She was standing with her ass rested up against the edge of her desk. He stood right in front of her and slowly slid his hand up her skirt and since she rarely wore panties his fingers quickly found their way to her womanhood. She started moaning and pushing his fingers deeper inside of her. "Don't stop" she whispered in his ear and he obliged. She really wanted to tell him to stop but it felt too good. Why the hell did he have to come into her office today with this shit? "I wanna taste you." He said licking his fingers. "Can you please let me taste you?" she knew she had to put a stop to this "Raymond we have to stop this." She said trying to turn and walk away from him.

"You don't mean that." He said as he wrapped his arms around her waist, pulled her to him, and began grinding himself on her to let her know how excited she was making him.

"Yes I do." She said almost in a giggle. He ignored her comment and worked his hands up around her 36 DD cups squeezing and massaging them. Unable to control herself she put her hands on top of his, closed her eyes and enjoyed the pleasure he was giving her body as he pressed his manhood harder on her rear end.

She didn't know why she carried on like this. If she had even thought Sean cheated on her she would flip out. In her twisted logic, as long as she didn't let anyone penetrate her she felt she wasn't really cheating. With her eyes closed and caught up in the moment she hadn't heard the door open but she did hear the flowers as they crumpled against the floor. Startled, she turned thinking that it was one of her co workers but instead she looked into the eyes of the man who just a few hours ago, promised to spend the rest of his life with her. At that moment Renee's whole world moved in slow motion as her heart virtually stopped beating.

"Oh my God." She said in a whisper turning back around.

"Don't you mean oh Raymond?" He whispered in her ear.

"Raymond stop." She said trying to break from the grip he held on her.

"You know you don't want me to stop." Raymond said in a muffled tone as he buried his head in the back of her neck inhaling her scent. His hormones blocked out all other distractions as he still hadn't realized Sean was standing in the door way.

"I think she means it dog." Sean said stoically.

Raymond, now fully aware of the situation, left the room too embarrassed to say anything. He ran out of the office leaving Renee to clean up her mess.

"I thought I'd surprise you with lunch." Sean said, apparently still in shock.

"Baby, please let me explain." Renee said trying to fix her mess.

"Please don't. Look, I have to get out of here before I do something I might regret later." She started to walk toward him but he put up his hand in defiance of her attempt to engage him.

"Don't try and explain this, you can't. This isn't something I heard about, this is something I saw. I can't believe I was about to marry you." That last remark stung her. He spoke to her like he had just discovered she was some low class whore.

"You still want to marry me Sean. I made a mistake. I'm not entitled to a mistake?"

"Mistake, are you crazy? The only mistake around here was me giving you that fucking ring."

"Sean, you don't mean that." Renee's voice quivered

"Oh yeah, well I mean this. The wedding is off. There is no way in hell I would marry you after this."

"You don't mean that baby; you just need time to cool off." She loved Sean and she couldn't see him actually leaving her over this. It's not like she was fucking the guy. She didn't think this was worthy of canceling the wedding.

"I hope you learn something from all of this." He said as he left.

That was the last thing he said before he walked out of her office and out of her life. Renee had tried to call him all night but expectedly all she got was his machine. The first few times she had left messages, but as expected he didn't return any of her calls. She figured she would give him a few days to cool off before she tried calling him again. She was so hurt & exhausted, all she wanted to do was get in bed and put today behind her. After she finished cleaning up the mess from the previous night she ran a hot bubble bath. As she put one foot in the water to test it, her phone started ringing. At first she was going to let the machine pick it up but she decided to answer it just in case it was Sean.

"Hello"

"Were you asleep?" It was Constance likely calling about that married man she was sleeping with. Renee never understood how she got so involved

with a man that she couldn't have exclusively. It was one thing to sleep with a married man but another in itself to catch feelings.

"No, but I was about to get in the bath, what's up?"

"I was wondering if Summer said anything to you about the hair show?"

"Yeah she said she wasn't going."

"Why not, we go every year?"

"Connie, I really don't know why. I think she said something about David planning something for them a few weeks ago but I haven't heard anything else about it."

"Hold on." Renee was about to hang up when Connie clicked back over with another line ringing, more than likely Summer's phone by the third ring David picked up.

"Hello."

"Hi David its Constance is Summer home?"

"No, she ain't get home yet. I'll tell her to call you." And he hung up without saying goodbye.

"He is so fucking rude." Constance said annoyed. *"I don't know what is up with him lately but he is being a straight asshole."*

"I thought it was just me, he has been acting shady lately. When I asked Summer about it she said its probably because of the pressure of trying to have the baby, but I feel if she can be nice through all of this, then he can be nice himself."

"Exactly, I was just telling Reggie that tonight."

"You saw Reggie tonight?"

"Yeah, he stopped by."

"Oh so now you have him around Meagan? Who do you tell her he is?"

"First of all Meagan was asleep tonight. And I tell her he is my boyfriend when she is awake." She wanted to ask her why the hell she would allow her daughter to be around a man who was married and had a family somewhere else but she didn't have the energy tonight. Because of Constance her bath water had begun to get cold.

"Look Connie I have to go my bath is getting cold."

"All right, are you stopping by the shop tomorrow?"

"I'll have to see, I might be working late tomorrow. This is a busy time of the year for us. More people getting new carriers and we gotta make sure they choose us and not the competition." She felt like she was pitching a speech to one of her employees at work, which meant it was time to go. *"I'll talk to you tomorrow Connie, I have to go."* She hung up the phone before Constance could even respond. Renee was good for doing that to people. As she came out of her Ralph Lauren bathrobe, Renee's thoughts shifted back to Sean again. She was so upset with herself for letting that happen. She really did love Sean and wanted to marry him. She also loved having sex even if it didn't involve him. She had even tried to involve Sean some how but he wasn't into freaky things like threesomes at least not when it involved his fiancé.

Ever since Renee lost her virginity on her 16th birthday she couldn't get enough of it. Her parents of course tried their best to keep her away from boys by sending her to all girls' boarding schools virtually all her life. She hated attending those schools. Only during her Junior high school years was she allowed to go to regular co ed public schools and that only happened as a result of her mother and father divorcing.

During that time of going back and forth to court, Renee got swept to the side. This was why Summer meant so much to her. It was during the time that her parents were consumed in their divorce, Summer was there, almost like an angel. Renee had always thought Summer was beautiful, with her wavy hair and high cheek bones. It wasn't even her looks that made her so beautiful it was her personality. Summer had a heart of gold she just wished that she could one day be blessed with a child. Renee didn't want any children right now. She was on a career high. She was making close to six figures as an ad exec at the phone company and owned a two bedroom condo in Clinton hills, Brooklyn. She drove a silver 2007 Lexus RX350 that her boss Raymond gave her half the money to pay for so she owed no note on it. Renee was a full figured woman, who had the HAT syndrome; Hips, Ass & Tits at 5'9 she weighed 160 pounds that she carried in all the right places.

As she stood and stared at what was left of the bubbles in her tub her thoughts went back to Sean and she decided to call him one last time. The phone had rung four times before he picked it up. *"Hello."* Renee's heart was beating so fast, she didn't know what to say next. Here she stood naked, still shocked to hear his voice on the other extension.

"Are you still upset with me?" She whispered into the phone, she could smell him through the phone. *"I'm sorry about what happened today. It was a big mistake baby, and I swear on my life it won't ever happen again. I just hope you can find it in your heart to somehow forgive me."* Wow I must really love him she thought to herself. Here she was, damn near begging him to take her back.

"Renee, I thought we already got this straight at your office. The wedding is off. You can take the ring and make a bracelet or whatever you women do with the ring when the wedding is off. But whatever it is you need to do it."

She could hear the pain in his voice and decided she should just let it rest for the night.

"Where are you staying?"

"I'm at my place."

"Oh, I didn't know you still had it." She never thought to ask him if he gave up his apartment when he moved back in with her. She just assumed he did, since he had offered and was paying the maintenance at her place.

"Of course I still had it; all of my furniture is here, Renee. Didn't you ever think about what happened to all of my stuff? What, you thought I just gave up everything and ran to you. Or do you ever think about anybody other than Renee?"

"Of course I do Sean, don't do that you know I always think about your well being. You know how much I love you, I just figured you put the place back on the market." she couldn't believe she was on the verge of tears but here they were stinging her eyes. She was more upset with herself than anyone.

She should've known that he would stop by after last night. She knew he had the day off because she had left him sleeping in her bed. Yet she was careless enough to let him catch her, with her boss no less. He knew she wasn't going to quit her job and if they married. Could he live with the fact that she was working under the man that had gotten under her skirt.

"Renee, be real with yourself you don't love nobody but yourself. For the past two years you've been going on and on about us setting a date. Then the very morning following us finally setting a date I catch you in the arms of your fucking boss. You obviously never really cared about setting no fucking wedding date this was just another way for you to feel in control of a situation."

"I don't know what to say Sean. I knew I shouldn't have even called you tonight. There isn't anything I can say to explain or right the wrong I made today. I just wanted to let you know how sorry I was that it happened. I never wanted to hurt you in any way. Despite what you may feel or think about me right now, I do love you Sean."

"Yeah well I just got home and I'm going to bed so I'll speak to you another time." He didn't say he loved her back.

"Okay Sean, Goodnight."

By the time she went to get in the bath the water was ice cold which mirrored the pain in her heart.

...*Summer*

By the time Summer reached home, David was already gone as she figured he would be. For the past month and a half she barely saw her husband. She had stopped cooking dinner two weeks ago and he hadn't even noticed. Tonight, she even skipped picking something up on the way home. She decided she would make a sandwich before heading to bed. David had left a message on the refrigerator that he went out drinking with one of his co-workers. He worked Ad sales for a local radio station so he would often have to entertain clients or travel to different sales conventions. Lately, his work schedule seemed exceptionally busy. She couldn't wait to see his pay statement at the end of the month, as he must've raked in a sizable commission. While Summer ate her sandwich, she turned on the TV to keep her company. With her mother's recent death and her husband's busy schedule she had become so lonely lately. She had hoped having a baby would help fill this void of loneliness because her husband sure wasn't.

As she looked at the dishes piled in the sink, she became very annoyed. She almost called and asked him why he didn't clean up after himself. She told him time and time again to clean up after himself. But like always he didn't listen to what she had to say. After she cleaned up the kitchen she checked to see if she had any messages. There were none, so she headed straight to bed. It wasn't until after 2am that David got home. Again, he came to bed smelling as if he just got out of the shower. He must've showered in the bathroom downstairs before he came up, thinking this wouldn't wake her. But once again she couldn't sleep. How could she sleep when it was after 2 am and her husband wasn't home yet? At first she was going to say something, but she quickly decided against it. Now wasn't the time for that. She decided to deal with him in the morning. Right now she needed to rest; her doctor told her she shouldn't get her body levels unbalanced. She was advised to stay calm and relaxed as much as possible. Summer would've stood on her head for two days straight if that's what they told her would help get her pregnant. It was the ringing of the phone that woke her from her sleep at 7.15 a.m.

"Hello." She said half asleep. *"Hello."* She said again, only hearing breathing on the other end. Who ever this was had done the same thing yesterday morning. She quickly hung up. She looked over at David and watched him as he snored in his sleep.

She had met David through a recording artist his radio station was sponsoring a promotional concert for. At the time, Summer had been a personal stylist for the artist. David was one of those rare gentlemen that you didn't think still existed. The one who opened doors, pulled out the chair and said and did all the things a woman wanted. He was old school. When she first saw him, she wasn't physically attracted to him. He was lighter than she liked her men and a little on the slim side. The only thing that did attract her was his height and his charm. He stood at 6'2 and wore his hair in a close cropped Caesar. When he smiled at her she saw a perfect set of teeth.

When they first started dating she thought he was the perfect man. Of course she knew better now. Now she knew there was no such thing as a perfect man, only perfect illusions of a regular man. She learned over time that even if you think your man is perfect he would more than likely end up doing something so far out that it'll turn your world upside down.

Summer found out one winter night when David stayed out until the sun rose the next morning. She had been furious at his lack of consideration and respect. When he got home she screamed, cried and screamed some more until he slapped her so hard across the face she saw stars. The left side of her face had swelled and her light skin had been scarred physically and emotionally by the outcome. She had to have Constance run the shop for a week while she healed. Everyone wondered what happened to her, but she lied and told them she was going to visit her grandmother down south. This way she would keep them from visiting her at the house and seeing her bruised face. David apologized over and over again, swearing up and down he would never do it again. Summer accepted his apology and believed his promise.

A year and a half later he had maintained his promise of not hitting her again. However, every so often he would continue to keep late hours. For the past few weeks he had come home late several times including the past two nights. Instead of things getting better they continued to get worse. Summer decided to go and make breakfast before she left to open the shop. She usually opened up at 11:00 but due to the long weekend and the business that accompanied it she had her first appointment booked for 10 and it was already after 8:00. When she got downstairs she noticed she left the TV on in the kitchen last night. Twenty minutes after she got the food on the stove David came down fully dressed with his suitcase in his hand.

"Where are you headed this early on a Saturday?"

"I'm headed to Florida. I have a business deal I have to close."

"Florida! When were you going to tell me?"

"I'm telling you now ain't I? I didn't know about it until yesterday. A client I thought had signed some papers didn't so I have to head out there and get this done before Tuesday or we lose the deal and I lose my job." He said grabbing a sausage off her plate. "You didn't make enough for me?"

"When are you coming back?" she asked ignoring his question.

"Monday night."

"Monday night? You've got to be kidding me, tomorrow is the fourth."

"I know, weren't you and the girls planning to do something."

"No we weren't. I was planning to spend some time with you since I can't seem to catch up with you Monday thru Friday when you're getting home all hours of the morning."

"Summer don't start with me this morning."

"Don't start with you? Dave, you came home at 2 in the morning. Now you're telling me you are headed out to Florida on business the day before the Fourth of July, and to top it off you're not taking me."

"If I asked you to go you wouldn't. I know how busy the shop is for you right now. I promise you when I get back I'm going to make plans for us to take a vacation."

"Oh, and you think just like that." she snapped her fingers to emphasize her point. "I can just up and leave the shop when it's convenient for you."

"Exactly my point. Besides you're the boss, anytime should be convenient for you."

"Well I don't need to be flying anywhere. That can mess up my cycle and I can't risk that right now."

"Your cycle? Come on now Summer, why can't we just live? Why does our life have to revolve around a baby we don't even have yet." Now this was a discussion she didn't want to have with him.

"I'll see you when you come back." She kissed him on his cheek on her way out the kitchen to go and get dressed.

When she arrived at the shop Constance was already there with Meagan, who was at the nail station getting a manicure. Constance was sweeping the floor while Summer's 10:00 was under the dryer. Summer being ½ hour late was comforted by the fact she could depend on Constance to hold things down when she wasn't able to.

"Nice to see you could finally join us." Constance quipped looking at her fictitious watch.

"I'm sorry I'm late. I didn't get much sleep last night." she said while grabbing a bottle of water out of the refrigerator. She could feel Constance staring at her, so she decided to go over and play with Meagan a little.

"Hey baby what brings you here today?" Meagan was a pretty little girl. She had the complexion of a penny and sandy brown hair that was done in braids and beads all over. At 9 years old she was well educated in books as well as the streets. Her mother had taken all measures to ensure she could survive at all costs.

"My Granny wouldn't keep me today because mommy came and picked me up too late last night."

Now it was Summer who stared. How could she get her late when she went home early yesterday just so she could get pick the girl up?

"Constance, can I talk to you in the back please?" She headed to the back before Constance could even respond. As soon as they got to the back office she let in on her.

"How could you Connie? I let you leave here early mainly so you could pick that baby up on time and what do you do? You go and fuck your man on the way. What type of mother are you?" she knew that last part was uncalled for and she wished she could take it back.

"Look Summer, I don't know what's going on with you in your house and whatever it is, it's your business the same way the way I raise my daughter is mine. I don't need you or anybody for that matter telling me what I'm doing wrong or right because I'm doing the best that I can."

"You're right and I'm sorry." She felt so stupid.

"Now do you wanna talk about whatever it is that's bothering you?"

"David came home after two this morning and I haven't been able to get any sleep." She purposely left out the part about him going to Florida on a holiday weekend and her just finding out this morning.

"Two O'clock! Where the hell did he say he was until two in the morning?"

"He didn't to be honest with you." She felt so stupid and she knew that Constance was thinking the same thing. 'How could you be so stupid' was written all over her face. Constance always played the big sister role and Summer could feel a lecture coming on. "I can't believe you're standing here telling me you let your husband get away with staying out *all night*. His mistress must be one happy bitch."

"Mistress, come on Constance. I don't think David is cheating on me, I think he's having second thoughts about having a baby and he's afraid to tell me. So he's trying to keep his distance." She knew there was a big change in David's behavior lately but she honestly didn't think he was seeing another woman. Why would he cheat on her? She was beautiful, nice; she cooked for him, did his laundry, and handled their money all while running her business. She did know that she was putting a lot of pressure on him lately about having the baby, but she was going on 29 and her chances of having a baby were already slim. She didn't want age to be another strike against her.

"So answer me this, where do you think he's coming from 2 in the morning?"

"You forget what type of job he has. Sometimes his business dinners run late."

"Late is 11 or 12 even but two in the morning? Summer come on, even you should question that."

"Why, because that's something Reggie would do to his wife? Well, I hate to tell you this Connie but every married man is not Reggie. There are men who are loyal to their wives." She said while walking back out front where there were two customers waiting. It was now 11:00 and another person was walking through the door. Summer knew it was going to be a long day.

As she was finishing her first customer's hair, a delivery man walked in the shop with a dozen of white tulips.

"I have a delivery for Summer Johnson."

"I'm Summer." She said smiling. White tulips were her absolute favorite. All the ladies in the shop looked on in awe oohing and whispering how romantic it was to get flowers at work. Everyone that is except Constance who knew they were guilt flowers and not flowers of romance.

"Who sent them, David?" One of her elder customers Ms. Jenkins asked from under the dryer.

"Who else?" Summer said, replacing them with some flowers in a vase that were half dead.

"That's David, Mr. Romance for you." Constance said rolling her eyes.

What was her problem? Summer thought to herself. If he didn't send the flowers she would have something to say, he sent them and she still had something to say. When has Reggie ever sent her flowers to her job? Never. That's when she began to wonder if Connie was a little jealous.

"Well, I think they're beautiful Summer and it was very thoughtful for him to think enough about you to send them. I mean it's not like it's your birthday or anything. He sent them just because he loves you." Ms. Jenkins said while holding the dryer up above her head.

"Or because he's in the dog house." Constance added, giving Summer a 'you know he's cheating on you' look. She couldn't understand why Constance wanted so badly for her to believe he was cheating on her when she didn't have any real proof to believe that.

"Even if he is in the dog house that's a lovely gesture to say I'm sorry. Cause trust me, a lot of these losers will just look at you like you owe them something." Ms. Jenkins said sticking her head back under the dryer.

"Mommy what time are we going home?" Meagan whined to Constance.

"Meg, its only 1:30. We'll be here for some time before it's time to go." Constance said while blowing out a customer's hair. "Why don't you go next door and play a couple of the video games." She went in her purse and got her some change.

"I want to go home with Granny." She said while crossing her arms. She had on a red Marc Jacobs dress that Renee had brought her for her birthday two weeks ago with a pair of matching red sandals.

"Well Meg you can't go home yet, so please just take this change and go play the game for a little while." Summer could see Constance trying to keep her patience but slowly losing it. It was 97 degrees outside and the heat was starting to get to everybody.

"Meagan why don't you try calling your grandmother and see if she says you can come over. If she does then I'll take you myself."

"Okay, thank you God Ma."

"Don't thank her yet, you better see if ma will let you come over." Constance said hoping her mother would say yes as she watched her daughter run to the phone, beads bouncing all over her head.

"Your flowers are pretty Summer." Ecstasy said sitting in Summer's chair getting her track sewn in. Ecstasy was recommended to Summer by Honey. Many of her clients had come via word of mouth. Summer and Constance had pictures of all types of celebrities adorning their wall with a hair style that they had gotten done there. Strippers, rappers and basketball players would come and get their hair braided and styled. Constance had twice been featured in Hair magazine with one of her authentic styles. They were doing extremely well for themselves and the shop stayed busy but never too busy. They always made money because of their steady clientele. They went by appointments only until recently when Summer decided to take walk ins. The decision was made primarily because she recently took out a second mortgage to buy the property next door so she could expand the shop.

"Marcus never sent me any flowers anywhere." Ecstasy said rolling her eyes. "I mean, I had a couple of the guys down at the club bring me some flowers but that was about it. I ain't never see no delivery man and he hand me some flowers." Ecstasy continued while buzzing in the man selling bootleg movies & CD's. "Come here baby let me see what you got."

Summer looked up from her chair at the man coming towards them and stopped him. "No offense but this is my shop and I don't go for bootlegging in here, can you please leave?"

"I'm saying, let me just holler at shorty right quick and I promise I'll be out." He said talking demonstratively with his hands. She knew he was just trying to make a dollar, but because of her various connects in the music industry she knew first hand how the artist suffered because of people like him and didn't want to support it in her shop. She made a mental note to speak to Ecstasy about it. She paid the man for two CD's and he left. On his way out Meagan came from the back office.

"Granny said she is on her way out the door." She said while flopping down in the chair.

"Well, what do you want me to do Meg?"

"I'm bored here, there's nobody for me to play with."

"I told you to go play the video games." Why did she have to make everything so damn hard? She acts as if I can just up and walk out and if I did where would she want to go? To her granny's house so she could play with her cousins who were so bad Constance couldn't stand to look at them. They were the children of her younger sister Tamara. Tamara was 25 with three kids and an out of work husband. She lived on public assistance and had never worked a job a day in her life nor did she ever plan to.

As Summer watched Constance with her daughter she daydreamed as to what Heaven would look like now. She still hoped that one day she could be blessed with a baby of her own. She had to figure out a way to make David want this just as much as she wanted it.

"Summer, the phone is for you." Terri the manicurist said to her.

"Thank you Terri, I'll take in it the back." Summer went to her office in the back. All she could fit in there was a small desk that held a computer monitor, phone and file hanger. She also had Frog build her some shelves to hold her fax machine and different pictures of her friends and family. He also built her a small bookcase. Renee tried to front like she and Frog weren't together anymore but Summer knew the deal since she was still walking around with the man's ring on. Renee was in love with Frog and that was the bottom line. She may have done her dirt but her heart belonged to him and there was no doubt about it. She sat down and took the call.

"Hello."

"Hey."

It was David. She didn't know if she should be happy or sad that he called.

"I see you had a safe flight."

"Yeah, I'm a little jet lag so I'm probably going to turn in for the rest of the night."

"Okay." She said emotionless.

"You know, I was thinking when I get home we could take a little break and go somewhere. Maybe if we had some time alone and it didn't feel like we were having sex for a purpose other than for the love we share... I don't know, I was just thinking."

Her heart sank; she was pushing her husband away because of her obsession with having a baby.

"I'll see, maybe that would be nice."

"Okay, well I gotta go. I'll talk to you tomorrow." He said in a hurried tone.

"I love you."

"Mm hum."

"Excuse me?" What was that about? She thought to herself.

"Summer I'll call you tomorrow, room service is at the door." He hung up. She sat there holding the phone listening to the dial tone until she heard the busy signal. She walked back out to the front in disbelief over what just happened.

...Constance

When Summer came from out of her office she looked as if she was on the verge of tears. For the rest of the night Constance had noticed that Summer was rather distant. It was now 8:30 and they were both finishing up with their last customer, Jean. Constance's mother had finally given in to her granddaughter and picked her up around 6:30. Even though she felt bad about not spending too much time with her daughter, she was happy her mother came and got Meagan. It was Saturday night, a holiday eve Saturday night at that and she wanted to get out and party. "Summer what you and Dave got planned tonight?"

"Nothing." She said in a low tone. What is up with her? Constance thought answering her ringing phone.

"Yo."

"Who the hell got the line tied up at the shop?" It was Renee, being demanding as usual.

"Nobody's on the phone Renee, are you sure you dialed the right number?"

"Don't ask me stupid questions unless you're a stupid person who only wants stupid answers."

Constance was tempted to hang up on her.

"Hold on let me check the line." She picked up the phone in the shop and it was dead. *"Something is wrong with it, I'll call you back."*

"Don't bother I'm on my way." Renee said before she hung up.

"Summer, did you hang up the phone in the back?"

"What?" She said looking up at Constance with tears in her eyes unable to hold onto them anymore.

"I said can I see you in your office please?" She said while grabbing Summer by the arm on their way to the back office.

"What's going on Summer?" She asked her as soon as they walked in.

"Nothing." Summer said wiping her eyes with a half hearted smile.

"Nothing?" Constance said walking towards the desk grabbing the receiver from the phone that was just laying there where Summer left it off the hook.

"You didn't even hang up the phone! So I'm going to ask you again, what is going on?" She said as calm as she could.

"I don't know. It's probably just my hormones messing with me." She was wiping her eyes again as she stood there lying to her best friend's face.

"What happened Summer? We have customers out there, I ain't got all night?"

"If I tell you, you have to promise not to say I told you so."

"Get real." She said sucking her teeth.

"All right for the first time in my marriage." She paused. "I think my husband might be having an affair." The tears dropped from her eyes as she said it out loud.

"I'm so sorry." She said giving her friend the hug she knew she needed right then. They stood there holding each other for a good two minutes. Summer broke it up saying. "All right we have to pull ourselves together and finish up." She walked to the mirror fixing her hair, which was short, wavy and bright red. Constance couldn't help but notice how much Summer resembled her mother.

Summer and Constance were listening to R. Kelly's Chocolate Factory CD singing along to the words of 'You Made me Love You' when Renee came tapping her manicured hands on the door which had the closed sign now lit up.

"Open the door, it's hot out here." Even though it was after 9 and the sun was finally set, the NY humidity made it feel like a sauna outside. Summer opened the door for her.

"You look like shit." Renee said to Summer as she grabbed at her.

"What's wrong with me?"

"I don't know you just look funny, like you need some sleep or something." Constance watched Renee as she tossed her pink logo Gucci bag in the chair. Ever the stylish one she also wore the matching belt and sandals. Her pink silk Dolce and Gabbana short set set off her hips while a pair of Gucci sun glasses adorned the top of her head. Constance eyed her outfit and wondered which trick she had buy her that outfit. Constance and Renee were only friends because of Summer. She always told Summer that Renee was too full of herself and if she wasn't in the picture there would be no way she could tolerate Renee.

"Well I look like shit because I'm stressed over the fact that I think my husband is cheating on me."

"Stop right there." She said holding up her hand. "We need to go out for drinks and discuss this."

"Now you're talking." Constance said as she now had a reason to wear the new outfit she brought from the mall last week.

"Let's go to The Lounge." The Lounge was a local spot that had a restaurant and bar upstairs and a dance floor downstairs. The Lounge was where she had met Reggie two years ago. Ballers and people from all walks of life shined at The Lounge.

Reggie was a lawyer at a well known law firm in midtown Manhattan. The firm gained notoriety amongst the African American community due to its works in high profile cases involving young African American males. Reggie was handsome and a dead ringer for Blair Underwood. Constance couldn't understand why he stayed married to his fat wife.

"We always go to The Lounge, let's go someplace different tonight." Renee said, swinging herself around in the chair to face Constance.

"Somewhere like where? I'm not in any mood to be trying different spots tonight. I really don't feel like going out at all." Summer said while looking at the floor. Constance really wanted to hug her friend. She felt so bad for her given the latest predicament. Constance peeped his card about seven months ago, so who knows how long he had been cheating on her.

"No, we're going out. I don't care if it's to The Lounge, it's the Saturday before the fourth so The Lounge is probably where's it's popping tonight anyway." Renee said standing up grabbing her bag. "So what time you guys wanna meet up?" She tossed her hair and subconsciously struck a pose.

"I really feel like just going home Renee." Summer said playing with her hands. Constance looked at her through the mirror she was fixing her hair in. "Go home and do what? You already said you didn't have any plans. Don't let David's tired ass stop you from enjoying yourself because it's not going to stop him." Constance said turning to look at Summer, pleading with her eyes for her to come out with them.

"Alright. But I'm bringing my car and when I'm ready to go, I'm leaving."

"Fine I'm taking a cab home because I don't want to drive drunk. Anyway after what happened to me yesterday I need a drink." Renee said opening the door. "I'll meet you at Summer's house around 11, later people." And she walked out leaving her familiar scent of Glow by J-Lo behind.

When Constance parked her 2003 Toyota Camry into the parking space she noticed moving men going in and out of her building. This could only mean they finally rented the apartment next door to her. It was a one bedroom so she wondered if it was a couple or a single person. Constance had lived there for four years and she hadn't planned on going anywhere anytime soon. The location was great as there was a park 2 blocks away and Meagan's school was only ten minutes from where they lived. She walked into the building praying she didn't run into any of her neighbors. She usually just held brief conversations with them so they wouldn't think of her as a bad neighbor. As she stepped on the elevator all she could think about was running into Reggie tonight. She really wanted him to see her in her new black mini dress. As the elevator doors opened on her floor the first thing that caught her attention was his eyes. They were gray and sexy; he had on a white wife beater that hugged against his sweaty chest. He smiled and moved to the side to let her off the elevator. She smiled back as they passed on his way onto the elevator. She turned and watched him as the door closed separating them.

"Damn he was fine."

Constance ran to her apartment to change. She was really ready to get her party on now.

...Renee

As soon as Renee got home the first thing she did was check her messages. There were three messages; two from her mother and one from her boss Raymond. She couldn't believe he had the balls not only to call her house but to also leave a message. Why hadn't Sean tried to call her yet she thought as she started to unbutton her blouse. She had sent him a large teddy bear with a card saying how sorry she was and how much she loved and missed him. She had it sent to his house because she knew if she sent it to his Construction Company his employees would embarrass him. She went into her bedroom and opened her walk in closet that was filled with all types of clothes and shoes. In the next closet she had coats, bags, belts and hats. She looked through her closet until she decided on a red Dolce and Gabbana linen jumpsuit with the back out and the breast cut in a dangerous V. The top tied up behind her neck so she decided to wear her hair up in a clip. As she picked out a pair of shoes to wear Renee couldn't help but think about Sean. He had recently become a constant in her life again and she felt incomplete without him there.

She was going to go out tonight and have fun to try and get her mind off Sean. A few bottles of Moet and she'd be fine. She couldn't believe that Summer had said she thought David was cheating. This meant all that time that Constance had actually been right about David. Damn, she hated when Connie was right because she was they type to throw it all in your face. As she stepped into the shower she had a sudden urge come over her. As she showered she removed the head from the shower and changed it to the jet stream. As the hard warm water massaged her clitoris she called out Sean's name.

Just as Renee had expected, The Lounge was packed. There were actually more people there than she expected. The line was half way around the corner. She was glad they decided to come here after all. On their way they had drove by a few other spots but decided not to go inside because the lines were either too long or too short. They had all met over at Summer's house where she learned that David was 'out of town'. As much as she loved Summer she had to admit, the signs were glaring. Summer was just too caught up in her own world to notice. Tonight she was noticing something. Summer had put on a white dress similar to the infamous

Marilyn Monroe dress where she's standing on the grate and it blows the dress up uncontrollably. She wore a pair of white sandals that strapped and wrapped up around her legs almost like a ballerina shoe with heel and sex appeal. She had her hair moused and styled which made the color stand out even more. Constance shocked them all with her micro mini dress made of Lycra material which hugged and grabbed every part of her body just right. She wore a lavender knitted shawl with matching bag and shoes. As they walked to the front of the line, Renee in lead, everyone looked. Renee with her cocky attitude walked straight to the front of the line. Frog's God brother Sheldon was a partner at The Lounge so they always had easy access. As they walked through, Renee noticed that there were not a lot of people inside. Not enough to have that long line outside. That's how the clubs got you. They made you stand outside to allow the line to build up resulting in an artificial buzz to all passerby's. Then, they gradually began to let people in, only after raising the door prices.

"Do you want to go upstairs?" Renee yelled to them over the loud music. She just wanted to sit down. She paid $852.67 for the shoes she was wearing and they were killing her feet.

"Yall go ahead, I'm going to stay down here." Constance said with a big grin on her face. Renee looked at her thinking *what has you so happy?*

"Looking for somebody?"

Without answering Constance stuck out her tongue and danced into the crowd.

When they reached the top of the landing, Renee noticed that most of the tables were occupied. There were a few tables in the back with reserved signs on them meaning you had to buy two bottles of champagne to sit. She headed directly towards the table. As she sat down she scoped the place out to see if she recognized anyone.

"Who are you looking for?" Summer asked her with a sly smile on her face.

"The waiter, I'm thirsty." She lied while grabbing her throat. "Did you see the line outside? Damn. I'm happy we don't have to go through shit like that."

"Do you think David is having an affair?" Summer asked abruptly changing the subject. Renee looked at her and thought what to say next as she didn't want to hurt her friends' feelings. "It doesn't matter what I think Summer. What matters is what you are going to do if he is." Renee said while signaling the waiter that she was ready.

"I don't know what I'm going to do. David is my husband and I love him." She said with pain in her voice. "Do you think the pressure of me getting pregnant chased him away?" After putting in an order for a large buffalo wing platter and a bottle of Moet she turned to her friend who sat there with sad hurtful eyes.

"Summer, you said it best when you said David is your husband. He knows how important starting a family is to you. So if he cheated on you because you wanted to get pregnant then he's a complete asshole." Renee said touching her lightly on her hands. It made Renee upset that Summer hurt like this.

"Here comes Frog!" She heard what Summer said but wasn't prepared for it. She hadn't seen him since that day in her office. She turned to look and saw sure enough he was headed straight for their table, greeting people along the way. Her heart skipped beats seeing him again, smiling. She loved him more at that minute than she ever loved him before. He was looking sexy in a black short sleeve Lacoste shirt and matching shorts. By the time he reached their table the waiter was just leaving. Sean gently took the bottle from Renee's hand and opened it for her.

"Thank you" She said, too afraid too look him in the eye as he placed the bottle on the table.

...Summer

Summer was happy to see Frog was there because she really wanted to just go home. The only problem was Renee didn't look happy to see Frog. Usually she would have hugged or kissed him by now. She knew Renee couldn't still be trying to put up a front like they weren't together, because she had been greeting him in front of Constance and Summer for the past few months. She also noticed that Frog hugged and kissed her when he said hello but didn't dare touch Renee. It was obvious something was going on.

"So what brings you ladies out tonight?" Frog said flashing his killer smile. That man could charm the pants off of any women in that place tonight he was in love with Renee.

"We just needed to get out tonight." Renee said almost in a whisper.

"All right then, enjoy yourselves." He said about to walk off.

"Are you leaving so soon?" Summer stopped him, seeing he clearly was not trying to sit down, which meant she would have to stay.

"Yeah, I have things to do." He said kissing her on the cheek. "You be good." He said looking at Renee.

"You too." She said looking at him holding her glass in her left hand. The light from above shone off the glass causing her ring to sparkle. As he walked off Summer noticed the hurt in her friend's eyes for the first time that night. Something was up all right. She had just been too caught up in her own world to see it. She was careful not to say the wrong thing to Renee because she was the type to clam up and not say anything if you came at her the wrong way. Summer poured herself another glass of champagne and they both sat there drifting in their own thoughts.

"What the hell are you smiling at?" Renee asked.

"Nothing. Why'd Frog leave so fast?" She asked grabbing a wing.

"I guess he has an attitude. Who cares he's not my man anymore." She said rolling her eyes thinking that would mask her pain. It didn't.

"Renee, who do you think you're fooling?" Summer said laughing. "Everybody and they mama knows that you and Frog are back together. Just last week we were here and you guys went home together. So what's up?"

"Nothing." She said tearily as she downed the last of her drink. It was more serious than Summer thought because it wasn't often that Renee cried, especially over a man. She got up from her seat and went around to the other side of the table and sat next to her friend.

"Renee, don't lie to me. What's going on?" She could see the pain hiding behind her friends' eyes as she poured herself another drink. She took a sip before she finally spoke. "We finally set a wedding date." Summer was confused why setting a wedding date would cause her so much pain. "Isn't that a good thing? I thought that's what you wanted." She took another swallow of champagne before speaking.

"The day after we set the date Sean caught me and Raymond in my office fooling around and called the wedding off." She raised the glass up this time finishing its contents. Summer just sat there too shocked to speak. She stared at Renee waiting for her to say she was just joking. She didn't.

"You're serious."

"Of course I'm serious. Do you think I would joke about losing my man." The alcohol had caused her words to begin to slur. Before she could say anything else Constance came over and joined them at the table.

"Let me find out yall ain't going to come downstairs and dance." She said sitting down pouring herself a glass of Champagne.

"We'll be down later Connie." Summer said still holding onto Renee's hand.

"I saw Frog walking through the crowd, did you see him?" Constance asked drinking her champagne.

"Yeah we saw him." Summer said as Renee drank another glass of champagne to keep the tears from falling.

"I want to go and dance." Renee said standing up now too drunk to feel the pain from her shoes.

"Are you sure Renee?" Summer asked, clearly concerned with her friends condition. She knew Renee wasn't big on dancing.

"She said she wanted to dance, you need to come with us too." Constance said pouring herself another glass before she headed back downstairs.

"No I'm about to leave soon." Summer said hoping they wouldn't protest her feelings but she knew better than that.

"Leave. Why are you leaving, we just got here?" Renee said a little tipsy.

"Because I didn't want to come in the first place, I would rather be home eating ice cream, watching a movie." Summer said gathering her things.

"All right then are you going to be okay?" Constance asked but Summer knew all Constance wanted to do was run back out on that dance floor and watch the front door hoping Reggie would show. She did it every time they came there. "Yeah you go ahead I'll call you tomorrow." Renee walked Summer out to her car while Constance went back to the dance floor.

"You're not to drunk to drive are you?" Renee asked as they walked arm and arm to her car with nothing but the sound of their heels hitting the concrete between them. "I'll be fine." Summer smiled at her friend. "It's only a feeling it's not like I have proof." She tried to laugh it off. "I know it's not like you walked in on him and another woman fooling around." Renee said with a half laugh. "Why was I so stupid? I should've made sure the door was locked. I've gone over this shit a hundred times in my head and I keep coming up with the same answer. I fucked up big time." She said still walking with her head held high.

"It'll be all right. Frog loves you; he just needs a little time to get over this."

Summer said as she deactivated her car alarm. She couldn't wait to get home. "All right Summer let me get back to the club before Connie thinks I left her." She hugged her friend and headed back to the club. Summer sat in her car and watched to make sure she made it safely back inside all the while thinking, "Damn, she did fuck up big time."

...Constance

"Before I let you goooooo oh, I would never, never, never, never let you go before I know." Constance sang along to the Frankie Beverly classic as the party reached its climax. She didn't even realize Renee was on the dance floor until she saw Frog come and snatch her off for dancing too close to some guy. She was shocked Renee even attempted something so bold. Despite Frog's attempts to keep her tied down Renee continued to do her thing.

Constance was thirsty and she debated on either going to the bar or upstairs and getting some champagne. She decided it best to go to the bar and get a drink. She would just order another glass of champagne because she didn't like mixing liquor. As she stood trying to get the bar maids attention she could feel the presence of someone watching her. When she turned around there they were again, those gray eyes and that smile. He stood there in a black shirt that showed off the muscles in his upper body and a pair of jeans. She wondered how he got in the club with those on. He stood there pointing at her gesturing to see if she was the same person from earlier. She tilted her glass and smiled back to acknowledge that she was and walked off. As fine as he was Constance was there tonight to dance, release some stress and if she was lucky, run into Reggie.

As she found a table to enjoy her drink she watched the crowd and finally, after all her waiting, Reggie finally walked in. Except she wasn't expecting him to walk in with another woman on his arm. Definitely not with a woman that wasn't his wife. "This motherfucker." She said to herself aloud. She debated her next move. Should she make a scene or should she just bounce? Damn, she couldn't just leave without telling Renee, who was upstairs with Frog doing who knows what. As she watched them they headed upstairs themselves. Damn, she thought again. Her heart was beating hard and fast, her mouth was dry and her lips were getting chapped. Either way she had to go upstairs so she decided she would approach Reggie and see what his story was. She swallowed the last of her drink to calm herself down a bit and headed up the spiral stairs to the dining area.

As she reached the landing the dim lights mixed with the alcohol began to bother her eyes. By the time she got them focused, Reggie was headed straight towards her. He grabbed her by her arm and took her by the pay phone and bathroom area. "Look I know what this looks like but it's not what it looks like." Reggie said guilt clearly protruding in his eyes. Even though she didn't want to see it she knew he was lying.

"Why'd you have to bring her here? You know I hang out here Reggie, Damn." She said grabbing at her head. What if Renee saw him she would never let Constance hear the end of it.

"Connie, she's a client of mine. She was feeling down because her son may be going to jail. So I offered to take her out and cheer her up a bit, that's all." He tried his best to convince her. "You said it yourself. Why would I bring her here, because it's not a date. You know you're my one and only." He said while hugging her.

"What about Patty?" She asked feeling a little more relaxed.

"What about her? She's my wife. You are my lover and there is no other."

Maybe she was a client that he brought out to cheer up. She had never thought about him cheating on her before so why should she think any different now. "So why don't you introduce me to her?" Constance said looking him in his eyes as he started to chuckle.

"And say what? She knows I'm married Connie. Who am I going to tell her you are, my mistress? I don't think so. I have a reputation to think about. Do you know what could happen to me if my wife ever found out about you? Lets just say it wouldn't be pretty." He said in a whisper as people walked by. Constance didn't know what to say. She knew everything he said was true and it hurt her. "I know, you're right." She said as she no longer had the urge to party. All she wanted to do at that moment was go home. "I'm about to break out so call me when you get the chance." She walked away from him not looking back because she didn't want him to see the tears as they slowly crept down her face. She went to the bathroom to clean herself up and went to find Renee.

...Renee

As Constance approached, Renee barely noticed her as she was in a heated argument with Sean. "I don't care what you say you still had no right to come and snatch me up like that." She was upset with him right now never mind the fact of what she did the other day. He knew better than to embarrass her like that. There she was dancing to her favorite song by Frankie Beverly and Maze. She hardly ever danced because being up on a guy in a club always made her want to fuck them afterwards. But tonight she was feeling herself so she really didn't care. It could've been the champagne but what ever it was she was feeling it. Two minutes into the song Renee found herself in a sandwich with one guy behind her and one guy in front. Not more than two minutes after that Sean came and snatched the guy from behind her and pushed the guy in front of her so hard he almost fell on the floor. He then snatched her, dragging her by the arm up the stairs. People stared at them and the guy he almost knocked to the floor began mouthing off. Sean's God brother watched the events from his office and ordered security to kick both guys out.

"What's wrong with you? Why you always want drama?" Sean said talking with his hands. As she watched the anger grow in his eyes she knew he wasn't going to leave her like he said he would. If he really wanted to leave, why did he care so much?

"Me, you are the one causing scenes in here. All I was doing was dancing."

She said looking him in his eyes.

"Renee." Constance said interrupting them.

"What up girl. Are you having fun?" Renee asked, smiling at Constance. She didn't want her to think that there was anything wrong between Sean and herself.

"I'm about to leave."

"Leave!" Renee said rolling her eyes. "Leave for what? You're acting like Summer now. Yall are some party poopers."

"Chill out Renee. If the girl wanna go home let her. You all right Connie. You look like you just saw a ghost." Frog asked looking concerned. Connie had known Frog through her daughter's father long before he met Renee. She remembered when he used to run the streets terrorizing people long before he opened his construction company.

"I'm fine. I think I had too much to drink, that's all." Renee watched her as she lied through her teeth, never thinking that Constance was in need of a friend right now."

"Too much to drink my ass, you're leaving because you didn't see Reggie tonight, you ain't fooling nobody." Renee smiled as she took another sip of her drink.

"Believe what you want, I'm tired and I'm going home so goodnight."

"Do you need me to walk you to a cab?" Renee said getting up. As hard as she tried to play she had a soft heart and if she considered you family then she always looked out for you.

"No, sit down. I'll be fine. I don't want you have to walk back by yourself."

"You sure?"

"Yes I'm sure. I'll call you tomorrow." And she sashayed as she walked back down the spiral stairs.

Renee was alone with Sean again. As she watched him bop his head to the music causing his braids to bounce back and forth it made her all hot and horny inside.

"Wanna go to my place?" She said while placing her well manicured hands on his lap. As he removed it he looked her straight in the eye.

"You've got to be kidding me."

"Excuse me." She said hurt while rolling her eyes.

"Renee don't act like what happened didn't because it did. Yes I still love you, but right now I can't stand you either. I'm not sure if I can move on from that shit." He said taking his hand rubbing it over his face as if he was trying to get the thought out of his head.

"Look baby, here is not the place to talk about this." She said looking him in his eye for any sign of forgiveness. "I know you're going to need some time but I'm not going to let you just leave me."

"How can I ever trust you again? I mean you work with the cat Renee."

Why'd he have to even bring this subject up again? She thought they were headed toward moving past this chapter.

"What do you want me to do Sean, quit?" She shook her head causing her hair to bounce across her shoulders.

"Yep." He said to her with seriousness in his eyes as he said it.

"Maybe I *should've* left with Connie." She told him letting him know that he had crossed the line.

"Maybe you should've." He said pouring himself a glass of champagne. As she stood to leave she stayed just a second longer to see if he would give in. He didn't. So hard ball is what he wanted to play so hard ball is what she would give him. "I'm leaving." She said grabbing her purse off the table. She opened it and dropped $500.00 on the table. "Tell Marc I said keep the change." She walked away.

"Take your money Renee." He called out after her but she just kept walking. On her way down the stairs she saw Reggie and his female companion going up. "Reggie?" Renee said while looking at the woman he was with who looked to be in her early twenties. "Renee right, how are you?'

"I'm fine, you just missed Connie." She said still looking at the girl.

"Did I? Oh well tell her I said Hi." He said trying to walk past her but she stopped him again.

"How's Patty, your wife doing?" She asked not caring how inappropriate it was.

"Come on Heather." He grabbed the girl as they walked past Renee, back upstairs to their table.

As she headed out the club the alcohol combined with the loud music was making her head spin. She still couldn't believe Sean had been so nasty to her. How could he think that she would even consider giving up her job because of his insecurities. Once Renee got outside she felt better. The humidity had subsided and the cool summer breeze felt good. As she headed toward 5th Ave to catch a cab she saw Constance as she got into somebody's Hummer and pulled off. "Let me find out this bitch is tricking." She headed to the corner and waived down a cab.

When she got home she kicked off her shoes, headed to her refrigerator, opened the freezer and looked for her chocolate chip cookie dough ice cream. She sat on her sofa and turned the TV on. As she flipped through the channels looking for something to watch at 4:30 on a Sunday morning besides paid for TV ads she entertained the thought of quitting her job for Sean. When the phone rang.

"Hello." Who could be calling at this hour?

"I just wanted to make sure you got home safe." Sean said

"Yes I did."

"You didn't have to run out like that. What did I tell you about driving drunk?"

"I took a cab home."

"So why didn't you tell me you didn't drive, I would've drove you home."

"Stop it Sean, okay. First you go off on me talking about you can't stand me. Now you're telling me I should've let you bring me home."

"I also said that I still love you which I do so I just wanted to make sure that you made it home safe."

Why was he doing this to her? It was either he wanted it to work or he didn't. She didn't have time for this back and forth.

"Well I'm home, so I'll talk to you later." She hung up before he could get another word out of his mouth. The same mouth she imagined pleasuring her as she masturbated herself to sleep.

...Summer

When Summer got home she was overjoyed. Being out in a club wasn't what she was feeling tonight. She wanted to go home and rest herself. She'd been up since 7 that morning and it was now after 2am. As she entered the foyer of her house she felt a strange feeling come over her. She always felt that her mother was with her somehow trying to communicate with her. She turned on all the lights in the downstairs area as she always did when she was home alone. She wanted anybody outside looking in to know that somebody was home. She went upstairs to her bedroom took off her clothes and got into her pajamas. She changed her sheets, washed her face, and then found her way to the kitchen. Her appetite had picked up over the past few days but she just brushed it off as stress. She found some left over spaghetti and heated it up as she turned on the TV in the kitchen. She noticed the message light on the phone blinking indicating she had a message. She hit the play button as she got her food out of the microwave. "**YOU HAVE ONE NEW MESSAGE. MESSAGE RECEIVED SATURDAY 11:47 PM BEEP: Ahhh fuck me, fuck me Daddy, oh yeah Daddy do it like that.** It was a female voice but who's and why did they leave this message on her machine. She was about to press stop when. **Ahhh David I love this dick. Fuck me harder David, fuck me harder.** Then the line went dead. She played it again to make sure she heard what she thought she heard and she had heard it loud and clear. What was going on? Who was that woman and was she talking about her husband David? Her unwillingness to accept the truth had clouded her rationale. What other David could she have been talking about? Her husband had now given her proof that he was having an affair. But with who and why? Was it because she wanted to start a family? How could she start a family now knowing he was unfaithful? So many thoughts ran through Summer's head as she begged herself not to cry. She had to stay focused so she could think as clearly as she could right now. she finished her dinner then she washed the dishes and put them away. After taking this time to calm down she decided to call her husband's cell phone. It went to voice mail and she opted not to leave a message. What was she going to do? What would she say to him, what would he say to her? Her phone rang and startled her. She was afraid to answer thinking it may be the caller again. *"Hello."*

64

"Were you asleep?" It was Constance, she was so relieved.

"No I was just about to head upstairs now. what's up?"

"I'm home."

"So early, are you feeling okay?" Summer asked wondering why Constance called her at 3am. Surely not to tell her she was home.

"Is it okay if I came over? I really need to talk to somebody."

"Can't it wait until the morning?" Was she ever going to get to bed?

"It could but I could worry myself to death by then."

"Fine then come over." She said giving in.

"You got any popcorn?"

"Popcorn! Girl do you know what time it is?" All she wanted to do was go to sleep.

"Yeah, like we use to do when we were kids we can sleep in the guest room and eat popcorn in bed. Remember that time when my mother caught us eating it and you told that Aunt Connie gave it to us. We was mad at you boy. Damn, I really miss her."

Summer knew something was wrong once she started reminiscing at three in the morning.

"Well hang up and come over, it's not getting any earlier you know."

What the hell. She thought she didn't have to open the shop up for the next two days anyway. Her eyes kept darting to the machine as she kept hearing the woman calling out her husband's name in an intense moment of sexual pleasure. She could barely get him to touch her lately and here this woman was screaming out his name. She had no idea what she was going to do.

...Constance

When Constance got outside of the club she felt like dying. Her heart was heavy and it must've been written all over her face because...

"Hey, are you all right?" He asked. She turned and looked at him thinking, *"Is this motherfucker following me?"* Every time she turned around there were those gray eyes. "I'll be fine. If you don't mind me asking, who are you?" she watched him as he laughed at her question.

"My name is Derrick, if that's what you mean." He said smiling showing his well paid for teeth.

"Derrick, huh well Derrick, why is it every time I turn around you're there?"

"What, do you think I'm following you?"

"Are you?"

He started to laugh at her again. As she watched him this time she thought, he was pretty cute for a white guy. Aside from gorgeous eyes he had beautifully tanned skin and a well shaped muscular body.

"No, I'm not following you. I just moved in your building and my boss at my new job told me about this place. His peoples have some type of connection to the place." Damn he has some pretty lips Constance thought as she watched him speak.

"What's your boss' name?" She managed to ask.

"Sean." He said flicking the cigarette he was smoking.

"Sean, that's my home boy! I've known him forever. He's even engaged to one of my best friends." She said not believing how small the world was.

"Really, it's really a small world after all." He said laughing.

"Yeah" she said rubbing her arms from the night air.

"Were you heading home? I can give you a lift, I was about to go myself." He offered.

"Sure why not." She could keep 30 dollars in her pocket. She was impressed when she saw him pop the alarm on the black Hummer.

By the time she got home she learned that Derrick had moved to New York from Columbus, Ohio 5 years ago. He was a plumber from a family of construction workers. He was 32 single, no kids and never married. He would've been perfect had he not been white. Not that Constance would've been interested in him if he wasn't white; she was just too involved with Reggie to see the good in another man. When she got inside of her apartment she felt the pain of seeing Reggie creep back up on her. She laid on her bed and tried to cry it away for about fifteen minutes before she decided to call Summer and see if she would let her come over.

It was 10 after 4 when she pulled into Summer's driveway. She laughed to herself noticing that Summer had ALL the downstairs lights turned on. She always did that when she was alone but at 4 in the morning she was attracting more attention then diverting it. Maybe they both needed company tonight she thought as she rung the bell. Summer opened the door in her pajamas and slippers. Constance had an extra pair herself waiting in the guest bedroom in the top draw. "Don't look so happy to see me." She said as she walked into the house.

"It's after four in the morning Constance, I'm sorry." Constance walked in past the family room, shaking her head as she passed.

"So why weren't you asleep when I called if you're so tired?"

"I had some things on my mind I needed to sort through." She said looking away. Constance sat on the stool near the island in the kitchen.

"Has Renee called you?" Constance asked.

"No, call me for what?" Summer asked putting the popcorn in the microwave.

"I don't know to tell you she made it home safe."

"No, she didn't call me. Why is everything okay?" She asked as she poured herself some juice. "Do you want some?"

"No" Constance said drifting back off to earlier. She still couldn't shake the feeling that Reggie was likely lying to her.

"I'm going to go and change into my pajamas. I'll meet you in the bed okay."

"Okay." She said taking the popcorn out of the microwave.

When Constance entered the room the first thing that hit her was the smell of the fresh flowers Summer kept in a vase on the dresser. They called this room the spare room, but it was really her room. She spent so much time over there that she had clothes in the closet and draws. As she opened the draw to find her pajamas Summer entered the room and climbed in the bed.

"So what has your mind all tangled?" She asked popping some popcorn in her mouth.

"I saw Reggie tonight." She said while taking off her clothes.

"Okay, what's so bad about that?"
Constance put on her pajamas and got into the bed before she continued.

"He was with some woman." She said stuffing popcorn in her mouth.

"What? Who did he say she was?" Summer asked shocked.

"He said she was some damn client he was taking out to cheer up."

"Well do you believe him?" Summer grabbed her hand to prevent her from stuffing another handful of popcorn in her mouth.

"I don't know what to believe anymore. I know I love Reggie and I don't think I can let him go right now." She said meaning every word of it.

"Constance, how could you want to hold on when you are hurting so much because of him?"

"I know Summer, but I love him. I can't help who I love."

"Does he love you Constance? I mean come on; he brought another woman to the club where we hang out."

"He has an exclusive membership at The Lounge. It's easy for him to get in on a busy night like tonight. Where else would he have taken her?" She said trying to convince herself more than Summer.

"If it's that easy why are you over here four o'clock in the morning crying?"

"Because I needed a friend, but if I'm bothering you I'll leave." Constance said redirecting her anger.

"Whatever Constance, I'm going to sleep." She turned over and went to sleep leaving Constance with her own thoughts. All the while Constance tried to make excuses for everything that went down.

The phone rung, thinking it might be Renee saying she got home, Constance answered it. *"Hello, Hello, Hello."* The phone went dead.

"They didn't say anything, did they?" Summer asked looking at Constance.

"No, but I'm about to *69 they ass." It rang 6 times before David's sleepy voice answered.

"Hello."

"Yes, did you just call here and hang up?"

"What? Who is this?"

"David?" Constance asked confused.

"Yes who is this?"

"It's Connie."

"Is everything okay, where's Summer?" He asked now fully awake with concern in his voice.

"She's here. I'm over your house. Your phone just called here but nobody said anything and it hung up." What the hell is going on? Constance thought to herself.

"Oh I'm sorry I must've been laying on it and it dialed the number back… I fell asleep with my clothes on. Tell Summer I'll call her in the morning." And he hung up. Now she knew something was up.

"It was David's number, how weird is that?" she said getting back in the bed.

"David? Why would he call here and hang up?" Summer asked as she naively shifted in the bed.

"That's what I want to know. What type of phone does David have? Isn't it a flip phone?" Constance asked trying to get to the nitty gritty.

"Yeah, what does that have to do with anything?"

"Everything because he told me that he slept on his phone and dialed the number back. You can't do that with a flip phone, he's lying." She knew he was up to something and now it was coming to light.

"Where did David go anyway?" Constance said wondering why she didn't mention anything of him leaving town before today. Usually when he left town they would make plans for a girl's weekend at her house.

"Florida. And I really don't feel like getting into all this right now."

"Closing your eyes and going to sleep is not going to change the fact that your husband is having an affair."

"I know that Constance. I'm not denying the fact that my husband is having an affair. I'm tired and I want to go to sleep. Staying up talking about this mess isn't going to change the fact that my husband is having an affair either so goodnight." A break through Constance thought. At least she didn't try and defend the fact that he was in fact having an affair. Constance decided to drop it for the night.

...Renee

When Renee rose the next morning she had a terrible hangover. She slipped on her Victoria's Secret slippers and robe and headed for the kitchen to find something to eat. It was now after one in the afternoon and the message light on her machine was blinking. She opened the refrigerator and pulled out some eggs, onions, green and red peppers and a few other items to make an omelet. As soon as she put the pot on the stove her cell phone started to ring. "Who is calling me this early?"

"Hello."

"Well it's about time?"

"Hello father." She had been avoiding him for a week now.

"How is everything going?"

"Everything is good I've just been working a lot with the holiday being here."

"Yes happy fourth of July to you. What do you have planned for today?"

Not spending it with you Renee thought to herself. *"Summer's having a barbecue today over at her house."*

"I thought you would come and spend the day over here at the house."

The house. She couldn't stand "The house" or the people in it. When her father divorced her mother it came out that he had another woman on the side. He divorced her mother and married a white woman, and moved her out to Long Island in a big house. Renee couldn't stand going over there for the summer. One plus of being away at boarding school was that she didn't have to deal directly with her nutty parents. When she was home she would spend half the summer with her father and the other half with her mother.

"I'm sure you guys will get along fine without me. Is Tabitha inviting any of her friends and family over?" Tabitha was her half breed sister. They were 12 years apart so they weren't too close but close enough to say I love you and mean it.

"Friends, what friends? If you're talking about those idiots in that band she plays with I don't think so."

"Daddy you need to open up a little. This isn't the seventies anymore."

"I don't care what year it is. There will be no boys in my house. Especially not the ones that look the way they do." Tabitha was in a R & B group called Radical that at best could be described as "eclectic". Tabitha was the lead vocalist and "face" of the group.

"Daddy, you need to give them a chance, they sound really good."

"Tina Turner sounds good, Gladys Knight sounds good, they're just making noise." He always knew how to kill a dream. *"Daddy, my food is burning."* And she hung up and went to finish making her breakfast.

After she finished eating and cleaning up after herself she headed back to bed but not before taking some aspirin for her headache. It was now going on two o'clock and she hadn't any idea what she was going to do today. Like magic her cell phone started ringing again. *"Hello"*

"Hi it's me, can you talk?" It was her boss Raymond. Why in the hell was he calling her on a Saturday?

"Yes Raymond, how can I help you?"

"I um... don't quite know how to say this." What was this babbling idiot talking about?

"Say what?"

"Is everything okay with you and your boyfriend?"

"He's my fiancé and that's none of your business. So what is it you're calling about?"

"I um I went to the doctor and found out that I have syphilis."

No the fuck he didn't just say that to me.

"So why are you calling me? We used condoms I know you're not saying I gave you syphilis."

"Renee, besides my wife you're the only other person I've slept with."

And like I said we used condoms Renee thought.

"Well did you ever think that maybe your wife gave it to you? If you're cheating on her what makes you think she isn't cheating on you? Besides we always used condoms."

"Always Renee?" Damn, she thought. He's right, there was one time when she didn't have any on her and she let him go raw dog because she was so horny. That was almost a year ago. She hadn't had intercourse with Raymond since. *"Look, thank you for calling and informing me. I'll make an appointment to go to my doctor and I'll call you when I get the results."*

"Fine that's fair enough."

"And Raymond, it's over between us. Don't call me anymore and I won't call you. This has just gone to a whole other level." She hung up on him just as he started to protest.

Syphilis, how gross! What if he gave it to her or worst she gave it to Sean. The only other person she slept with without a condom was Sean and she hated to even think that she could've gave it to him. Now her head was hurting for a different reason. She was calling her doctor first thing Tuesday morning when everything opened back up after the holiday. Renee decided to go to the gym and work off some of her stress.

74

...Summer

When Summer woke up the next day she felt much better. Constance was already awake downstairs making breakfast. She could smell the bacon in her sleep. She couldn't remember the last time she slept so well. It was a quarter to two when she glanced at the clock as she brushed her teeth. All the while she was thinking about that message on her machine. She also thought about what happened last night. Why would David's phone dial the house and hang up. All signs were pointing to another woman. What would her mother think at a time like this? As she headed downstairs she prepared herself for Constance.

"Good morning." Constance said in a surprisingly good mood.

"Good morning. How are you feeling today?" Summer asked pouring herself a glass a juice.

"Much better, funny what a good night's rest can do for the soul." She got up and made Summer a plate of food.

"So, have you decided what your next move is going to be as far as he's concerned?"

"Not really, I mean he did explain the situation so I'll just see what his next move is and then play off of that."

As they finished their breakfast reading the paper it was Summer who broke the silence. "Connie, I'm going to tell you something but you have to promise not to overreact." She was not in the mood for Connie and her opinions on what she should do with her marriage, she just needed somebody to talk to right now.

"What's up? Does this have anything to do with last night?" Constance asked placing the paper to the side.

"To be completely honest, I'm not sure myself. Last night wasn't the first time that someone has called and hung up. Usually when they call David is here, so for the call to have come from his phone kinda threw me." Summer said watching Constance before she continued. "Then last night when I got home, this was on the machine." She went over to the answering machine and played the message. When the message was done she saw the anger build in her friends' eyes. She knew Constance was about to go on one of her 'I knew he was cheating' rants but instead she calmly said. "Who ever this woman is, she wants you to know."

"Why do you say that?" Summer asked her while getting up to make a cup of tea.

"Why? Summer, don't continue to be so blind. Do you think that message was a mistake? She is calling your house over and over. She probably called last night from his phone hoping you would call it back." Constance said rolling her eyes in anger.

"Why would she think I would call back this time, I've never called back before. Shoot, I kinda thought it was a prank caller so I paid it no mind really until last night."

"Because she knew by then you had heard the message. Think Summer, the signs have been there for a while, you've just been too caught up to see." Summer knew it was coming.

"No, I've been too busy to see it. I mean I do have a business and a house that I have to tend to."

"Yeah and that's why your man has been running around with another woman."

"Something you know all too well."

"Yeah it is. That's why I'm trying to school you. Who ever this woman is she is trying to get you out the picture so she can have David to herself."

"You think so?"

"Why do you think she wants you to find out? She wants you to leave him so he could be with her. Who ever she is she's desperate to go to the lengths she has gone."

"But why?" Summer asked pouring water into her tea cup.

"Shit, why not? Who knows what David is doing for this woman? He's probably treating her better than she has ever been treated in her life and now she thinks she's in love."

"In love! Do you think he's in love with her?" Summer never thought about that.

"Can't say, I'm sure he has feelings for her just based on the time they've been together but you never know."

"How do you know how long they've been together?" She wondered if Constance knew more than she was letting onto.

"Summer, I told you about my suspicions almost 6 months ago. Who knows how long it's been?

"Well what you thought doesn't mean he was seeing her that long." She couldn't believe she was sitting at her kitchen table in the house she and her husband shared discussing how long he'd been seeing another woman. It was starting to sink in that it might already be too late to save her marriage.

"Yeah you keep thinking like that and by the time you realize what's going on you'll be served divorce papers." She got up from the table and went to get dressed. As Summer sat there thinking about her next move she called Renee but got her machine. She left a message for her to call her back as soon as she got back in. She needed to find a way to save her marriage and she needed to do it fast. She needed her girls.

...Constance

When Constance went upstairs to get dressed she didn't know if she was more upset with Summer because she was being the stupid wife or because whoever David's mistress was, was doing a hell of a lot better job than she was doing as one. She got in the shower got dressed and headed home. She didn't have to go and pick up her daughter until later tonight after the fireworks. As she parked her car her cell phone started to go off.

"Hello."

"Hello sexy." Her heart sank, it was Reggie.

"What do you want?"

"You sound upset. I know you're not upset." She wanted so badly to be upset yet she was so happy that he called. She had been thinking about calling him since she woke up but fought the urge.

"Should I be?"

"Upset for what, I told you she was just a client. You're my lover and there is no other. Now can I have a kiss?"

"No." She wanted to string him along just a little longer.

"No, so what if I take it." Before she could respond he knocked on her car window. He scared the shit out of her. She couldn't contain the smile that came across her face as she rolled down the window.

"What are you doing here?" She beamed with happiness.

"Waiting for you beautiful, where's Meagan? At your mom's?" He said looking just as good as he wanted to. His bald head shining in the sunlight. He had on a polo shirt and short set with a pair of sandals. He got in the passenger side of the car.

"What are you doing?" She asked laughing as he leaned over and took the kiss he asked for.

"Would you just shut up and drive." He wiped the lipstick off his lips.

"Where are we going?" She wiped where he missed.

"Just drive. I'll give you directions as we go." She did what she was told.

He ended up directing her to a co-op building in downtown Manhattan where he had access to a loft. The place was absolutely beautiful; Constance had never seen anything like it. The borders around the ceiling matched the pattern on the bedspread as well as the upholstery throughout the room. The bathroom had a Jacuzzi and the balcony had a scenic view of the east river.

"This place is beautiful Reggie." She said checking the place out.

"I was hoping you would like it." He grabbed her in his arms. "I get to use it from time to time on my company's account. Tonight is a perfect night to be in a place like this. There's a great view for the fireworks." She felt warm inside knowing he had brought *her* to a place like this on the Fourth of July. "I was hoping for some different fireworks." She said unzipping his pants and dropping to her knees to show him just how much she missed him. After they finished up they laid there, hot and sweaty.

"Isn't this nice?" she asked still smiling.

"Huh, yeah it's nice." He said dozing off.

"Are you falling asleep?" she asked shoving him. "We have this beautiful room on a day like today and you're going to sleep. We haven't even tested out that Jacuzzi yet." She said. He turned over saying.

"I'm tired, make sure you wake me at 6." He went to sleep.

She got up and decided to take a shower, after the shower she sat on the balcony in her birthday suit and smoked a cigarette. The summer breeze felt cool against her naked body. She was so caught in the moment she didn't notice Reggie until he started to caress her breast from behind. She grabbed his hand and held her head back as he leaned over and kissed her. She wondered how a man could kiss her with so much passion and not want to spend the rest of his life with her. "I thought you were asleep." He took her by the hand and led her back into the loft. Once inside she tried to kiss him but he pushed her away. "What's wrong?" she asked skeptically.

"I'm leaving. You can stay if you want, just make sure you lock the door when you leave."

No he didn't. "Leaving? We didn't even see the fireworks." She couldn't believe he was doing this to her again. Every time she thought they were moving forward he would put everything on pause. He stopped getting dressed long enough to look her in her eyes.

"I know you're not getting serious on me Connie. You know I have a family. It's the Fourth of July; surely you know they're expecting me?" Even though she knew he was right she was hoping that he was some how coming around. She didn't want him to see this weakness so she laughed it off.

"Of course I'm not. I don't know I just thought… forget about it." She walked back out on the balcony feeling naked on the inside as well as the outside.

...Renee

As Renee hit the Stairmaster at the gym, she couldn't get the phone call out of her head. She pumped her legs extra hard as J-Lo's 'Waiting for Tonight' played in her ears. As she eased her steps she could feel someone staring at her. Not wanting to be bothered she decided to get off the machine and head towards the sauna room. Whoever was watching her was now following her. Aggravated, she turned around to be met by a sexy specimen of a man. Damn, she thought to herself as she returned the smile that he threw her way. He had on a wife beater tee shirt and a pair of work out shorts that fit in all the right places. As he got closer, he tilted his head pointing at her, never letting go of that smile. "Renee?" He said as if he wasn't sure it was her. Who the hell is this? She wondered as she nodded yes.

"I'm sorry, do I know you?" She replied, trying to place his face.

"It's Terrence, from Howard." He said as if that would help her know who the hell he was. She had slept with so many men during her time at Howard; this guy could have been anyone. If she did sleep with him he sure didn't look like this. She would have been sure to remember him.

"I'm sorry, I don't remember you. Were you in one of my classes?" She asked as she wiped sweat from her brow with her towel.

"No, I was never that fortunate to be in one of your classes. You use to date my Frat brother, Zeke." For a minute, even that name didn't ring a bell.

"Right, Zeke I haven't seen him in years, how is he?" she asked not really interested in the answer. Zeke wasn't the sexy ass standing in front of her.

"Well to be honest I haven't spoken to him since I got kicked out of school." He replied with a chuckle. Renee stood there admiring his demeanor and physique. His arms were chiseled and she couldn't help but admire the soft curls on the top of his head. His chocolate skin was two shades darker than hers and blotch free.

"Damn, I haven't thought about that in years. So what's been going on with you?" He asked tapping her lightly on her shoulder.

"Ah, a little bit of everything. Look I hate to be rude but I'm heading to the sauna and I have to be out of here soon so..." Before she could finish he interrupted her.

"Well look, why don't I give you my number and we could try and hook up sometime." As cute as he was Renee was trying her best to go the loyal route.

"I don't know Terrence." As she said it, a disappointing look came across his face.

"I understand." Looking in his eyes, she changed her mind.

"Well, I guess it won't hurt if we were to hook up at some point."

His smile returned. "Cool, wait right here while I grab a pen."

As he walked away Renee couldn't help but blush as she watched his ass. Had he caught her on the street he might've known that she was engaged, but since she took off her jewelry to work out he was none the wiser.

...Summer

As Summer cleaned her house she couldn't help but shake the feeling of hurt, pain and betrayal. She devoted her life to her husband and in return, he cheated on her. As the phone woke her out of her trance she was afraid to answer it thinking it might be the woman from last night.

"Hello." She whispered into the phone.

"Hi it's me." It was Constance.

"What's up? Is everything cool?"

"Everything is fine. I just wanted to invite you down to this loft I have for the night. It has a great view of the east river so we'd be able to get a good view of the fireworks."

Summer could hear a faint hint of disappointment in her friend's voice.

"Who do you know with a loft with a view like that on a night like this?"

"Reggie, he got it for me. Are you going to come through or what?"

Reggie got it? What the hell was going on?

"I guess, do you want me to call and invite Renee?"

"Sure, if she doesn't already have plans."

"Okay, so where are you?" Constance gave Summer the address and directions and they hung up.

Before she could dial Renee's number her phone rang again.

"Hello."

She answered thinking it was Connie calling back.

"Hey baby happy fourth of July." It was David her heart sank and she wanted to hang up the phone.

"You're just now returning my call?" She had called him almost 4 hours ago and left a message on his voice mail.

"Yeah, I was caught up in something." Rather in someone Summer thought. *"Yeah, well I'm on my way out the door."* She couldn't believe the love she had for him was turning to hate so quickly.

"Where are you going?" He asked sounding pissed off because she was going out.

"Out." She spat at him. If he was really concerned he would be at home with her.

"Well I figured that much, but where?" he said softening the tone in his voice.

"When you're home then you can ask me shit like that. Until then, don't question me." She said finally standing up for herself.

"Excuse me? You are still my wife whether I'm in town or not." He said his voice quickly rising in volume.

"Well, as your wife I would like to know who called my house last night?" she asked raising her voice to match his.

"I told you that was an accident. I fell asleep on my phone." He lied.

"Yeah, well like I said, when you're here then you worry about what I'm doing because when you're not here I have to worry about who you're doing." The words came out of her mouth before she could stop them. She didn't want to have this conversation over the phone. She wanted to wait until they were face to face because of how easy it was to lie when you didn't have to look your accuser in the eye.

"And what is that supposed to mean? Let me find out you are letting Connie fill your head with that nonsense." He tried to redirect the blame.

"Whatever David, I have to go." She hung up before he could get another word out. She felt relieved standing up for herself against him. It was about time that he knew that she was no longer going to play the "dumb wife". She grabbed her car keys and headed out the door to do a little shopping, deciding to call Renee from her cell phone.

...Renee

"Hello" Renee was feeling good. Running into Terrence at the gym had given her something to keep a smile on her face. She hadn't met any new guys with some potential in a while.

"What's up, you busy?" Summer asked

"Nah, I'm about to go in the building. Why do you have me on speaker phone?" She asked with an attitude.

"I'm driving Renee. I don't want to get a ticket. You know how the NYPD is. Anyway, Constance has a loft overlooking the East river for the night. She's inviting us over to watch the fire works. I was thinking we could order some food, you know make it a girl's night."

Since when could Constance afford a loft over looking the East river, not to mention it was the Fourth of July.

"Really, where'd she get a place like that on a night like tonight?" Renee questioned with a hint of jealousy in her voice.

"She said Reggie got it for her." Summer replied. Now Renee was really confused. Why Reggie would rent a loft like that for Constance was beyond her, especially after she just saw him in the club with another chick the night before.

"Reggie? Why would he rent Connie a loft?" She wanted to go just to see the look on Constance's face when she told her about what went down last night after she left.

"I don't know Renee but he did. Are you coming or not?" Summer asked a bit annoyed with Renee's unnecessary questions.

"Yeah I'm coming, where is it?" Summer gave her the address and directions and they hung up. When Renee entered her building, her doorman had a package for her. She could tell from the box it was roses

which meant it was more than likely from Sean. When she entered her apartment she went straight to the shower. The whole time she showered she thought not of Sean but of Terrence. She imagined what his lips would feel like against hers; she yearned to feel the warmth of his breath as she anticipated their first kiss. The ringing of the phone interrupted her thoughts and she stepped out the shower and answered on the 5th ring.

"Hello."

"Did you get the roses I sent you?" It was Sean. She knew without even opening the box that they were from him. He always sent her flowers when he felt guilty about something and the way he treated her last night was well worth the flowers today.

"I did." She answered a little tired of the routine. He was so predictable.

"Did you read the card?"

As much as she loved Sean, meeting Terrence and agreeing to hook up with him had made her question if she was really ready to get married.

"No Sean I didn't."

"Why not?" He asked changing the tone of his voice obviously disappointed.

"Sean, do you think you can talk to me however you want and some flowers will make it all disappear, well it won't." Not this time she thought to herself. This time she was ready to take a break. She was tired of the bullshit with him. What happened last night wasn't even as big of a deal as she was making it. She blew it up because she wanted to start seeing Terrence without a guilty conscience.

"What are you doing tonight?" He always did that when she was mad. He just changed the subject like how she felt didn't matter. She almost hung up on him.

"Sean, I think we need to take some time apart from each other." There, she finally said it.

"What? What do you mean by time apart? After what I caught you doing you have the nerve to tell me you need time from me. Time for what? So you can fuck your boss without a guilty conscience." Damn, he knew her so well. Only, this time it wasn't her boss.

"No Sean, because of your attitude about my boss whom might I add I'm not fucking."

"Yeah, sure you're not. You think I don't hear about the shit that goes down. Come on Renee we run with the same people. This may be the first time I've said something but it's not the first time I've heard it."

She couldn't believe what she was hearing. What did he know and why was he just bringing this up? If he knew, why was he sticking around all this time?

"Well, tell me Sean. What have you heard? If you know so much why are you with me? Sending me flowers, what the fuck is really going on?" She said on the defensive side.

"That's a good question. I guess when it gets right down to it I loved you. I didn't want to believe what people; who I felt were jealous of us thought. I felt just because a person is flirtatious doesn't mean they are fucking everything moving. Guess I was wrong. You want space no problem, I hope you enjoy that." Click.

She opened the box of flowers which was an assortment of roses in every color. She opened the envelope with its Hallmark symbol indicating that he more than likely dropped the roses off himself while she was at the gym. *You are the pot of gold at the end of my rainbow. Love always Sean.* Inside the card was the money she left at dinner last night. She couldn't wait to get dressed and address the one person she knew was responsible for spreading her business.

...Constance

Sitting on the balcony watching the people arrive for the fireworks spectacular only added more pain. Watching the couples arrive or the parents set up chairs and spaces for their children only made Constance wonder what Reggie was doing. Worse, what he was doing without her. She couldn't understand how a man she loved so much could love someone else. She went inside and slipped on the Gap summer dress she had laid out on the bed. She was hoping that after the fireworks they could go out and party a little. As she was slipping on her shoes the bell rung letting her know it was show time.

She didn't want her friends to know how miserable she felt inside so she ran to the bathroom to check her make up and made sure her massacre hadn't run from the tears she shed earlier. She opened the door and greeted Summer who was the first to arrive. "Hey girl did you find the place okay?" she asked stepping back letting Summer into the apartment.

"Yeah, your directions were on time. Damn, look at this place! Its lovely in here." Constance smiled inside and out for the first time since Reggie left.

"Thank you. I said the same thing when I first saw it." She said smiling, feeling renewed that he let her have the room for the night. "I like your short set." Summer had on a white Marc Jacobs halter top one piece short set with a pair of white sandals that showed off her freshly painted red toe nails. She was sporting a pair of Burberry shades that Renee bought her that sat perched on the top of her head.

"Thank you, I picked it up today." She said as she headed toward the balcony. "I can't believe this view. It's great." She said as she looked down on the crowd that started to develop. Constance fixed them a drink and when she joined her friend on the terrace she could detect that something was wrong. "Summer you okay?"

"I'm fine. It's just seeing all these families down there hurts a little. Knowing that all I want is to have one and my damn husband is destroying it before it even starts." She said taking the champagne from Constance.

Constance bit her bottom lip. She felt her friend's pain but at least she had a husband to start a family with. She swallowed the champagne in her glass in one gulp.

"Did you get in touch with Renee?"

"Yeah she should be on her way. She called me while I was on my way over and said she was leaving."

As much as Constance loved Renee she couldn't understand how she was able to get the things she got when she treated everyone like they were beneath her. The only person she ever saw her show any respect towards was Summer. "I'm surprised her and Frog didn't plan anything for tonight." Constance said while pouring herself another glass of champagne.

"I think something's up with the two of them. I'm not sure, you know how secretive she can be at times. David called this afternoon." Summer said as she walked back inside of the loft and took a seat on the couch.

"What did he say?" Constance took off her shoes just as the doorbell rang. "I knew that was going to happen once I got comfy." She went and opened the door for Renee.

...Renee

As soon as she entered the lobby her blood pressure rose ten degrees. She couldn't understand why Reggie would put Connie up in such a beautiful place. When Connie opened the door for her she saw the look of pure jealousy come across her face. Connie's eyes looked admiringly at her pastel blue Ralph Lauren silk summer dress and her Jimmy Choo sandals. She carried a small clutch bag and her eyes were hidden behind a pair of Chanel shades. Reggie may have put her up in this place she thought to herself as she looked around, but she was still the flyest bitch up in it.

"Damn, you just walk in and don't say hi. I didn't sleep with you last night."

That was Connie with her big mouth.

"Of course you didn't that's why you woke up in this beautiful loft." Renee said as she removed her shades. "So, how much ass did you have to put out to get this spot?" She added for the hell of it.

"Not as much as you did to get half the shit you got on." Connie said as she rolled her eyes and sipped her drink. Renee wasn't in the mood especially since she hadn't had anything to drink yet. So, she let her little comment slide for the time being.

"You look cute Summer, I like your hair like that."

"Thank you. You don't look too bad your damn self. You got a date tonight?"

Summer asked.

"No, not tonight. I thought we might be going out after the fireworks." She responded while pouring herself a drink. "What time do the fireworks start?" She asked Constance while grabbing a seat next to Summer.

"Nine or ten, I'm not sure. I have the room till tomorrow though. So it's on like popcorn." She said doing a dance. Renee couldn't help but smirk as Constance spun around in her cheap ass summer dress. *I bet she think she looks cute.*

"So where is Reggie at? He just gave you the keys and bounced." Renee asked ready to start trouble.

"Yeah, he was here earlier in the day but he had other plans for the night." She responded obviously hurt so Renee decided to press the issue.

"Other plans with whom, his wife?" She sipped her champagne before she continued. "Or the girl I saw him at the club with last night?" She gave Constance a 'Did you know about that?' look. Much to her surprise Constance didn't even flinch.

"Oh, you met her too. She's one of his clients' mother. She was down so he decided to take her out to try and pick up her sprits a bit." *So she knows about the chick in the club.* "So whose Hummer did I see you jump into after you left?" She knew shit wasn't as sweet as Connie tried to make it seem.

"You saw that? That's the guy from my building that moved here from Ohio. He actually works for Frog." She saw the look in Constance's eyes saying you don't know everything you think you know. She decided she'd lay off for now and focused on why her friend had looked so down. "Summer why do you look so sad?"

...Summer

She was surprised Renee even noticed her mood amidst her childish rant with Constance. For the life of her she couldn't understand why they argued the way they did. It was so stupid and unnecessary. They were friends and right now more than ever they needed each other.

"You mean other than my husband having an affair."

"Why would you say something like that? Just last night you said yourself that you didn't have any proof. Are you letting Connie fill your head with that other woman mess again?" Renee asked.

"Me? I'm not the one who left a message of her man fucking some chick on her answering machine. Maybe if she *had* listened to what I said a long time ago she would be over his sorry ass by now." Constance said starting to feel the effects of her drink. Summer shot her a searing look. She always had to take it an extra step. How did she know if she wanted Renee to know about that phone call.

"Well now I guess you know the truth, the whole truth. Somehow, I assume it was David having sex with some woman and it got recorded on my machine." Summer said as she shook her head as if it could erase the memory.

"That could have been anyone. Why would you assume it was David?"
"Of course it was him. The bitch called his name out during the phone call and then called later that night from his cell and hung up on me." Constance said further airing out Summer's business.

"Damn, why would the bitch call you? I thought you mistresses liked to stay a secret." Renee said to Constance indicating she wasn't helping the situation. Summer stood up and poured herself another drink. She didn't want to ruin their girls night with her problems.

"Look ladies, I don't want to talk about this anymore. The fireworks will be starting soon. I decided to hire a private investigator, so we'll see what he finds. Until then let's just drop it.

"You didn't tell me you were going to do that?" Constance said looking upset. For some reason Constance hated not knowing things before Renee.

"Maybe she didn't want to tell you. You act as if she has to tell you everything. As negative as your attitude is, it's a wonder she tells you anything." Renee said raising her voice.

"Negative. You have the nerve to call somebody negative when all you do is use men. As good as Frog is to you, you flirt openly with other men. He finally set a fucking wedding date and what do you do? You get caught fucking around with your boss. How positive is that?" Constance said clearly showing she had too much to drink. Summer wanted to stop them but it was already too late. As soon as she heard Constance say it she knew it was too late.

"You jealous bitch! I wouldn't be surprised if you wanted to fuck Sean your goddamn self. You probably already did." Renee said with hate in her eyes. "Don't play yourself Renee you're the only whore in the room. You probably don't even know how many men you've been with." Constance said raising her voice.

"If I didn't I bet *you* do. All you do is admire me. You want to be me so bad it fuckin' kills you. And know that I'm aware of you running behind my back like some fucking 9th grader telling Frog what I was doing. Like the saying goes misery loves company. Just because that married man won't leave his wife for your broke ass you had to try and destroy my happiness." Renee screamed as her hair danced across her shoulders. Summer looked at Constance with shock. She hoped that what Renee just said was a lie.

"Constance you didn't" Summer asked looking Constance in her eyes for a sign that it was a lie.

"Of course she did. She doesn't want to see anyone happy. You of all people should know that by now. She's so miserable I can't even be mad at her. Look at her sitting there with that raggedy ass dress on. That's the difference between you and me baby. If I was fucking a high price attorney he would be paying but you're so concerned with somebody trying to love your stupid ass you get nothing." Renee said as her chest heaved up and down from anger.

"Bitch if I get nothing what the fuck you doing here? This shit was arranged by *my* man." Constance said trying to mask the hurt she was feeling.

"Don't make me laugh. Your man, please. If he was *your* man *he* would be here with you right now, not us." Renee said fuming mad as she watched the hurt come to Constance eyes.

"Bitches like you kill me. The only reason you got half the shit you got is because you fucked for it. You ain't fly bitch, you just a high priced hoe." Constance said with hate in her voice. "I almost feel sorry for *your* ass. You'll never know what it's like to have a man love you for you."

"If you feel sorry for me you better feel sorry for yourself. Because if you think for a second that Reggie loves you, huh you better think again." Renee said as Summer pleaded with her eyes for Renee to stop.

"How the fuck you know he doesn't love me? Are you in his brain?" Constance asked with one hand on her hip.

"I know because when the motherfucker was trying to fuck me he told me so. Yeah bitch, the man you think loves you so much tried to fuck me on many occasions." Renee said matching Constance's stare with her own. All Summer could do was place her head in her hands because she knew it was the truth. She herself had witnessed this at least twice. The only reason they never told Constance was because they knew Renee would never do it. They felt there was no need to hurt Constance's feelings.

...Constance

No this tramp is not standing here in my face lying on my man. "First of all I know he would never be desperate enough to try and step to you because he knows that you ain't nothing but a slut."

Summer interrupted her before she could say anything else.

"Enough! All this name calling is unnecessary, we are friends. We are supposed to be here to have a good time, not fight with each other."

"Friends, that's your friend. I only deal with her because of you. I would never befriend a whore." She stared straight at Renee. She couldn't believe she would drag Reggie's name into all of this.

"Well you know what? You don't have to worry about me because I'm leaving. You can always tell when bitches aren't used to having shit because this is how they act. Summer, I'll talk to you later." And with that she left.

"Good riddance. Summer, you want another drink?" Constance said pouring herself another glass.

"No, I can't believe you just did that. How could you go behind her back and tell Frog things about her." Summer asked. Constance finished swallowing before she spoke.

"Oh please, I didn't go behind her back and tell him shit. He would hear shit and come and ask me if it was true. All I did was tell him if he keeps hearing all this shit then maybe it's true." Constance said not really caring. Renee was a flirt and everybody knew it.

"You shouldn't have even said that. That's not your place. That would be like her going and telling Reggie's wife that he was sleeping with you and then giving her your address."

Constance just looked at her. That was not the same.

"Why are you trying to defend her? All she does is think she's the shit. She thinks she can get with any man and take him for whatever she wants. In my book that's a hoe. I don't know what you see it as. And to think the bitch tried to say Reggie wanted her, please." Constance said as she sheepishly laughed at the thought.

"I don't know why that's so funny to you. Instead of worrying about who she's fucking you need to worry about who Reggie's fucking. Because if he can cheat on his wife, he'll cheat on anyone and that includes you." She grabbed her bag and left. As Constance sat there alone she realized how alone she really was. The explosion from the fireworks outside scared her, and as she watched them the tears slowly slid down her face. She had nobody. She wanted to call Summer and ask her to come back. She wanted to call Renee and say how sorry she was. Most of all she wanted to call Reggie and tell him how much she loved him. The intensity of the moment coupled with the alcohol caused her to run to the bathroom and vomit all her troubles away.

Part Two:

The Hell

...Summer

As she sat in her bathroom staring at her husband's monthly commission statement, her heart rate increased. According to his statement, he only took two business trips last month and that didn't include the Fourth of July weekend. Since he returned three weeks ago from Florida they had barely said a word to each other. He spent more time away from home and she started to care less and less. Last week she finally made good on her promise and hired the private investigator. David's decision to take another "last minute" trip last weekend was the final straw. The investigator had been trying to reach her for the past three days but she hadn't returned his call. After seeing this statement, she would be sure to reach him before the days end.

She hadn't heard nor seen much of Renee since the Fourth of July when she and Constance had their big blow out. She had stopped by the house last weekend to get her hair done because she refused to go to the shop. Summer had damn near begged her to let it go but Renee had her mind set. Ever since that day Constance had become distant. She would come to work, do her job and immediately head home. She hardly stayed late and her conversation focused on business only. It was as if overnight the nature of their friendship had changed considerably. Summer wanted so badly for them to reconcile, especially now that she was about to find out what the investigator had to say. She was thinking about calling Renee to join her but she thought against it. David knocking at the door interrupted her thoughts.

"Summer are you almost ready?" He asked.

"Yes. I'll be down in a minute, go warm up the car." She answered trying to get herself together. They were going out for breakfast this morning. He had suggested it last night during one of her crying episodes which began to occur more frequently as of late. He had come to realize their marriage was falling apart and suggested they try to start rebuilding. She wondered if it was already too late.

By the time they reached the restaurant breakfast was no longer being served, so they had to make it a brunch date. They went to a new restaurant where they were seated outside. "I can't remember the last time we sat down and ate together." David said, pulling out her chair.

"Thank you." She said sitting down. "I can't remember the last time we did anything together, anywhere."

"Well, lets try and make this the beginning of a new us." He said grabbing her hand. "You're still my Pumpkin."

"You just don't want to have a baby with me." She said grabbing her hand back from him.

"Come on now Summer, you know that's not true. I just don't want this to consume our marriage. It's like when it doesn't work out the way you want it to.. I don't, I just don't like seeing you hurt so much over this." He said looking her in her eye.

"What hurts me David is knowing my husband doesn't want the same things I want. It hurts me having to wonder if my wanting a baby is sending my husband to the arms of another woman." She replied

"Come on now Summer, don't be ridiculous. I will admit that all of the stress at home is causing me to spend more time at work but another woman... that's a bit much." He said taking a sip of water. The waiter came over and took their orders. The whole time Summer kept her eyes on him. How could he sit there and say he was working when she knew good and damn well he wasn't. His commission statement had confirmed that lie.

"So how are things at work? All these extra hours at work you must be trying to get a promotion or a raise. Maybe now I'll be able to cut back on some hours at the shop. All this overtime you're doing I should be able to expand sooner than later." She said laying it on extra heavy all the while watching him closely to see what he would say.

"Summer, taking the loan out was the best thing to do." He said watching the door.

"I know that. But with you working all these extra hours I'm sure to pay it off sooner than I thought." Her head had began to throb but she wasn't sure why. She had been getting headaches for the past couple weeks.

"Summer, the extra money I'm making needs to be put aside for the baby." No he didn't just try and cover up his lie by bringing up a baby that he acted like he doesn't even want.

"Baby? What Baby? We haven't even been having sex to make a baby. Now you want to save money for one." She said anger quelling in her voice.

"Is this what our marriage has come to? Has it gotten to a point that we can't even speak without arguing?" He said looking in her eyes.

"This is the reason why I work so much. You think I like all this fuckin' arguing." He said tossing his napkin across the table as people started to notice them.

"Don't you dare sit here and say the reason you work so much is because we argue. The reason we argue is because 'you work so much'." She said making quotes with her hands and fingers, refusing to back down from him. She was tired of his bullshit and she refused to sit here and let him blame her for the affair he was having.

"If it's not work, what do you think is keeping me so busy?" He asked looking at her in a daring way.

"I got a better question for you. What fucking business trip did you take on the Fourth that didn't show up on your commission statement? According to your statement you only left town on business twice. And if I remember correctly from June 15th to July 15th you took four trips. So tell me what happened to the other two? Were those for your side hustle?" A look of shock came across his face.

"You're checking up on me now? Is that what this is all about?" He tried to confuse her with his anger but she was ready for him today. It wasn't working.

"Why don't you answer the question David?" She said calmly.

"I went away to clear my head. Do you think I like being treated like a fucking machine? Sometimes I feel like all you want me for is my sperm. You don't love me anymore, you just covet the fact that I have healthy sperm. If my sperm was no good you would probably toss me." He said raising his voice.

"Don't make me laugh David. You are willing to make any excuse to hide the fact that you're having an affair. I'm not going to sit here and let you blame me for your insecurity. You're having an affair and not because I want to have a baby but because you aren't man enough to tell me you don't." Before he could answer she had to excuse herself to the bathroom. When she returned to the table, her food was there with a hundred dollar bill and no David. After she ate her food she called the investigator and took a cab to his office.

...Renee

As Renee watched Terrence sleep she wondered to herself how she had fallen for this guy so fast. During the last few weeks she had spent every available moment with him. It all started on the Fourth of July after she left the loft. As soon as she got in her car he called her on her cell phone. As she explained to him what happened he gave her directions to where he was and they had been rolling together ever since. Unlike a lot of her other relationships, she wasn't interested in what he could do for her. She just felt comfortable being with him. That's not to say that he wasn't earning his keep. In the past three weeks he had taken her to all of the hot spots and always had access to the VIP section. He loved showing her off to all his people. To him she was the epitome of beauty and she loved the way he made her feel.

Due to the fact that he just came up to NY from Virginia and was living out of hotels, she had allowed him to stay at her place temporarily. He had come up to New York to help produce an up and coming hip hop artist. Since Renee wasn't into Hip Hop, she didn't know who the rapper was nor did she care. In her eyes the only people who made money in that industry were the producers, so she was happy that he was producing and not performing. He would usually come in after catching late hours at the studio, sneak in bed and they would have sex for what seemed like hours on end. As she got out the bed she repeatedly thought *with the good comes the bad.* As much as she was enjoying him she couldn't stand the fact that he didn't clean up after himself. He would come in every night and drop his clothes on the floor as opposed to putting them up. This was something she loved and missed about Sean. He always helped her maintain and keep the house clean. She hadn't heard from nor saw Sean in the past few weeks. He had left messages for her a few times but after she stopped returning his calls he stopped leaving messages. One night when she and Terrence were returning home from a party she could've sworn she saw Sean's car parked with him sitting inside. She was too drunk as well as scared to turn around and confirm it, so she just let it go.

As she picked up Terrence's pants, she was curious as to what was in his pockets. He would normally empty them out, but last night he was too drunk to do anything. He barely touched her last night so she figured he was out of it. Her curiosity got the best of her and she reached her hand inside and pulled out its contents. He had about $200 in cash, keys, and a cell phone. As she dug further she found 5 small baggies with white powder inside. This last discovery came as a shock. Renee had dabbled with cocaine back in college so she immediately knew exactly what the powder was. She slowly placed everything back in his pockets as it was. "I can't believe this shit. Why didn't I see the signs? Now what the fuck am I going to do?" She decided to get dressed and go to the gym. As she got out the shower, Terrence was in the kitchen drinking OJ straight from the carton.

"I wish you would use a glass." She said rolling her eyes. She hated for people to do things like that. It was so unsanitary to her. "If they wanted people to drink from the container they wouldn't have made glasses."

"Good morning to you too." He said before burping

"Morning? It's 2'oclock in the afternoon." She went to her bedroom to get dressed. He followed behind her.

"What's your problem?" He asked, grabbing himself as he watched her put lotion on.

"Nothing." She said continuing to lotion herself up. The discovery of the drugs in his pockets had put her in a foul mood. He walked over to her and violently grabbed her head trying to force her to give him oral sex.

"Excuse me, what the hell are you dong?" She said jerking her head from his grip.

"What? I don't see you protesting when it's me doing you." He said becoming defensive.

"First of all, I have no problem doing you, but don't grab my fucking head. I'm not one of those groupies down at the damn studio. Not to mention I just got out the shower and I pay too damn much for my hair for you to grabbing on it like that."

"Groupie? Where did that come from? Did I ever say or do anything to make you feel like a groupie? And as far as your hair goes, your best friend owns the damn beauty salon where you get your hair done." He said climbing back in the bed.

"Exactly, it's her business, not a charity. She has to make a living and she can't do that by letting people get their hair done for nothing, not even her best friend. Which reminds me, when are you going to start getting a pay check?" She asked looking in the mirror applying lip gloss to her lips.

"Don't start Renee. I already told you I won't really see my paper until after this kid's album drops. Even then it's going to take some time. That's just how the industry works.

"So how do you expect to live until then?" She said turning to face him. She was now fully dressed. She wore her workout suit, sneakers and her hair up in a ponytail.

"Are you strapped for cash or something? Is there some new fucking outfit out you want to get?" He said sarcasm in his tone.

"Don't make me laugh. What ever I want I can buy for myself. I don't need you or any other man to buy me shit." She lied. Most of the things in her closet had been bought by a man in one way or another. She was now getting to a point where *she* was starting to feel used by Terrence.

"Then what the fuck is the problem?" He yelled.

"Nothing, just forget it." She decided to back down because the bass in his voice was not typical and it frightened her a little. "I'm going to the gym so I guess I'll see you tomorrow afternoon." She said as she walked out the bedroom. Before she could make it to the door he slid up behind her. He grabbed her from behind, pulled her close to him and started kissing her on the back of her neck while softly whispering in her ear.

"What's wrong with my baby?" He said lowering his hand down her shorts quickly finding her sweet spot.

"I said nothing." She answered resting her head on his shoulders as he sucked harder on her neck.

"It doesn't look like nothing to me." He took his free hand, unzipped her top and started to caress her nipples. She moaned out loud as he pulled her shorts down and worked his way for his tongue to join his hand and dance around inside of her. He then carried her into the kitchen, threw her face down across the table and hit it until she was loudly screaming his name. After they finished they laid there hot, sweaty and out of breath. The only thing she could think about was the fact that he had just ejaculated inside of her. She had just received a clean bill of health from her doctor and she had promised herself she wouldn't put herself in that predicament again and she just did.

...Constance

As Constance cleaned she sang along to the song playing on the radio. Today was the first day she felt a little like herself in the past three weeks. Even though the thoughts of the previous night haunted her, she knew she had to get over it and move on with her life. After Summer left, she was in the bathroom vomiting from all the liquor and excitement when she saw "it". As she was on the bathroom floor she looked up and saw a small red light in the drop ceiling. As she removed the tile she found a camera and followed the wire to a compartment in the living room. After jimmying the inside of a previously locked cabinet she found a DVD player, TV and various DVD's labeled with different women names.

As she pressed the play button her hands shook with fear when she heard the machine start up and play. She watched Reggie enter the room on the TV. She looked around realizing there must be hidden cameras all over the place. The woman with him on the screen was the same woman he told her was his clients' mother. She watched as they had sex in every part of the loft. From the bathroom to the kitchen to the living room. The sight of the video caused her to run back into the bathroom and throw up again. Only this time it wasn't from the alcohol, but from pure disgust. Once she returned to the video she saw herself with Reggie, screaming as he inserted her angrily. The look on his face proved that he knew they were being taped. She couldn't help but notice the smug look on his face as he looked into the camera. She had never felt more hurt in her whole life. How could she have been so stupid to get involved with and then fall in love with this man? She could only wonder how many other women he had done this to. According to some of the dates on the labels he was jumping off, on average twice a month. She grabbed the movie that featured her, fixed the place back up and left. On her way home she had felt so scattered and her heart was too wounded to think straight.

If only she hadn't been such an ass to her friends, she could've confronted them with this news. But she already put her foot so far in her mouth she couldn't dare share this information with them, she was too embarrassed. In a deep depression, she sent her daughter to stay with her mother for a few days. She was barely able to get out of bed to go to work and even when she was there she wasn't really there. However, today was a good day because Meagan was coming home and she couldn't wait. She had missed her child and needed her energy, spirit and companionship during this trying time. She hadn't spoken much to Summer, when they were at work she kept it on work. She knew Summer had no idea what was going on. She likely thought her attitude was from the argument they had.

The knock at her door took her by surprise since she was going to pick Meagan up so she knew it couldn't be her mother. Since the night she discovered Reggie's video's she had changed her number and would only enter the building after carefully surveying the block. She would circle the block at least twice to make sure he wasn't there. "Who is it?" She asked while walking to the radio to turn it down. While looking through the peep hole she saw Derrick on the other side of her door. Relieved, she opened the door and greeted him with a smile. "Hey."

"Hey? I'm glad you're in such a great mood this morning, but do you think you could turn your music down some? I mean it's only 9:00." He said looking at her with sleepy eyes.

"I'm sorry. I was cleaning and I usually listen to music when I clean."

"Yeah, well I just got home not too long ago and I'm really tired, so if you don't mind." He said emotionless. She couldn't help but notice how quickly he was adapting to the New York attitude.

"I see you're taking to the New York lifestyle rather well." She said to him.

"What is that supposed to mean?" He said looking confused.

"Your attitude buddy. Don't worry, I'll be sure to turn the music down and next time you knock on my door, you be sure to say good morning first." She slammed the door in his face before he could respond. *He has some damn nerve.*

...Summer

As she sat outside of the building she wavered back and forth about going inside. If he discovered something that she couldn't handle it might be too overwhelming. She almost decided to leave until she looked down at her wedding ring. She knew in order to save her marriage she had to know the truth, begin the healing process and then move on. There was no way to move on while living a lie at the same time. She gathered her things and headed to find out what the investigator had found. As she rode the elevator her heart was doing a little dance in her chest while she could feel the butterflies in her stomach. When she stepped off the elevator she was greeted with the aroma of fresh flowers. A bell chimed indicating a visitor had just entered the office. It was Sunday and all the staff must've been off. Mr. Jones opened the door leading to his office and led her inside. He was a tall slender man with a Jheri curl that he wore slicked back. He was wearing a black and gray jogging suit with sneakers.

"Hello Mrs. Johnson, I've been waiting for you. You are a hard woman to catch up with." He said holding the door that led to his office as she walked in.

"I know. I'm sorry, I run my own business so sometimes that takes up a lot of my time." She said showing a nervous smile.

"It's okay Mrs. Johnson. We're on the same side. I work for you." He said noticing the common jitters.

"I know, it's just this makes me so uneasy. I mean thinking your husband is having an affair is one thing but paying to find proof is another." She said as she sat down on the sofa in his office. His office was set up like a living room. There was a coffee table in place of a desk and sofa and loveseat.

File cabinets lined up against the wall were the only indication that this was in fact an office. She watched as he went toward the files and pulled out what must have been her file. She almost felt faint as he handed her the manila envelope. Her hands shook and started to sweat, she was so afraid to open it, so he took it out of her hands and did it for her.

"From the time you hired me I have come to find out quite a few things about your husband. He has very expensive taste. He flies first class, stay's in four star hotels while on vacation and spends an abundance of money going out to eat, shopping and the like." He still held the folder in his hand.

"Wait, you followed them while they were away?" she asked sounding confused. She didn't inquire on the fact that he referenced 'they' which proved that there was in fact another.

"Are you kidding me? Of course I did. This is what you paid me for isn't it?" He said matter of factly.

"I mean yes. I just thought you'd do a little snooping and that's it." She responded.

"Not for the fee I charge. Mrs. Johnson, when you come to me you get results. Whether they be to prove you wrong or prove you right you're going to get results." He said before he continued. "Now from what I gather, this has been someone he's been involved with for sometime now."

"And you know this because?" She asked.

"I know this because I've been doing this for a long time. You can tell from the way they interact with one another. When I show you the tape you'll be able to see what I'm talking about."

Tape, I didn't think I would see a tape.

"From your point of view, do you think they're in love?" She asked looking in his eyes to try and gauge if there was any way to save her marriage.

"My point of view doesn't matter. I'm here simply to do a job Mrs. Johnson." He said calmly.

"I see." She replied now eager to get this over with. He was starting to creep her out a little.

"Are you ready to see the photos?" He asked as he pulled them from the envelope. As he held the pictures her head began to spin. But she quickly gathered herself and shook her head yes.

"The first set I'm going to show you are the pictures at the airport. These pictures will show what I mean about them seeing each other for awhile. Usually when a couple is new they may board the plane separately or maybe take separate flights. But as you see they are very much together." He said as he handed her the set of pictures. The first one she saw was from the back. Even from the angle Summer couldn't help but notice how familiar the woman looked. As she flipped through pictures trying to get a glimpse of her face she couldn't since all of the shots were from behind. Some had the woman resting her head on David's shoulder's, while others showed them holding hands.

"Are there any showing this woman's face?" She asked curious as to why she appeared so familiar.

"Of course. However, since first class is board first I was only able to get them from behind. But I did get a few on the plane and a few of them entering the hotel after one of their shopping sprees." He said handing her the next set of photos. This time her hands didn't shake as much and she had begun to relax a bit. As the tension eased she wanted more. The first shot of them on the plane showed more her husbands face as the woman's face was turned towards the window. Her stomach turned as she watched her husband carrying on with this woman as if *she* were his wife. Vacations! She screamed in her head. She couldn't shake the feeling that she knew this woman from somewhere. As she approached the next few pictures of them entering the hotel her blood pressure boiled uncontrollably as she watched the woman in the picture laughing with her head held back, grabbing onto her husbands arm. As the pictures showed these two enjoying what seemed to be a lovely afternoon, Summer could only shake her head as she realized that this was in fact a face that she knew quite well.

...Renee

As she drove to the gym she couldn't help but wonder what was happening to her. Here she was letting a man that she barely knew live in her home rent free under the guise of good sex. She had dumped her fiancé, done away with her friends and cut off all her jump offs for a man that she barely knew anything about. She had turned her life in a different direction and she wasn't sure if it was for the better anymore. When she had first met him, she had enjoyed all the attention to keep her interested and she wondered if it was already too late to get out of it. She had moved this stranger into her home under the pretense that he could complete her life in some way but in actuality he was making it worse.

As she thought further, her pursuit of sex had once again clouded her judgment. A block away from the gym she spotted Summer hurriedly walking out of an office building visibly crying. She wanted to pull over but was caught in heavy traffic. By the time she circled the block Summer had already pulled off. She tried to call her on her cell phone but it went straight to voice mail. She left her a message telling her to call her as soon as possible. She then tried to call Constance but both her cell and house number had surprisingly been disconnected. Renee wondered what the hell was going on. Had she been so caught up in her own affairs that she hadn't noticed that everything around her was crumbling?

As she parked her car her phone rang. Without checking the number she answered. *"Hello."*

"You miss me yet?" It was Terrence checking up on her. She should've known it was him. He had a habit of calling a half hour to an hour after she left the house. It was almost as if he didn't trust her out of his sight.

"Not yet, is there something you need?" She said obviously annoyed with him and his smothering ways.

"I was just laying here and I realized I can still taste you." He said.

113

"So that means you still haven't gotten out of bed and it's going on 4 o'clock." She said expressing her disapproval at his apparent laziness.

"No, I actually just got out of the bed. You say that like it's a problem if I sleep late. Its not like I work regular hours like most people." He replied

"Well maybe you should. Two jobs never hurt anyone. Especially since the one you have now ain't paying and won't start until who knows when." She said sarcastically.

"Don't be a smart ass Renee. I'll see some paper as soon as this album blows up. Then you'll be all on my shit. But don't worry I'll leave a couple of dollars on the table for you before I go because it seems to me like I'm becoming a problem for you." He said with faint regret in his voice.

"It's not that, it's just... don't worry about it. Keep your money, as long as you're not asking me for any everything will be fine." She said giving in. As much as his free loading was getting to her she did care for him a bit and since she wasn't starving it made no sense to cause a problem. She decided to leave it alone.

...Constance

"Connect four" Constance yelled with excitement. She and Meagan had been home playing board games all night. Meagan had beaten her in every game but Connect four was one where Constance was finally getting the upper hand.

"You're cheating mommy." Meagan said becoming annoyed with the 3 to 1 score despite her winning all night.

"No I'm not. Did I say that when you beat me in Trouble and Bingo? Everybody runs out of luck sooner or later." She said as she pinched her daughters' cheek.

"But I'm not a cheater, you are." She said sticking out her bottom lip.

"No I'm not a cheater." Constance said a little defensive.

"Yes you are, that's what Grandma said." She said with wide eyes.

"Excuse me." Constance replied taken back by her daughters comment.

"Grandma said that you and Mr. Reggie are cheating on his wife." Meagan replied matter factly. Constance was so thrown by the comment that she didn't know what to say. "Well is it true, are you a cheater?" Meagan asked waiting for an answer.

"Come here baby." She took her daughter and sat her next to her. "Grandma talks about stuff she has no idea about. What's important is mommy is no longer seeing Mr. Reggie, and to answer your question. No, I did not cheat you in Connect Four I beat you fair and square." She tickled her daughter until she couldn't take it anymore. While she laughed on the outside Constance really hurt on the inside. She never wanted her daughter to look at her in a whorish way and she knew that only whores broke up happy homes. As she put her daughter to bed that night she made herself a promise that no matter how much she wanted to she would never see Reggie or another married man for that matter again. After her daughter fell asleep she ironed out clothes for the next day and sat down to watch TV when her doorbell rang. She got up to answer it sucking her teeth when she looked through the peep hole and saw Derrick.

"Let me guess my TV is too loud." She said moving her neck making her hair bounce from side to side.

"No." He said revealing a box of cookies from behind his back. "Peace offering. I thought about what you said before you slammed the door in my face. About me getting a New York attitude and I hate to admit it but you were right." He held the cookies out to her. She held her head down with embarrassment at both the gift as well as from what he said. She had only said what she said because of what she was going through, it was nothing personal.

"Thank you. Would you like to come in for something to drink? I have some left overs if you'd like." She said trying to make up for her smart comment.

"Thanks and as good as that sounds I really need to get to bed. I have to be to work at 6 and I'm sure you know Frog doesn't take very well to lateness." Constance looked at him and for the first time wondered what he would be like in bed. Heck, this was the first time she thought about someone other than Reggie that way in a long time and it made her blush.

"Yeah I heard how Frog could be." She said still blushing.

"But if you don't mind I would love to take some to go. I mean, I haven't had a good home cooking since I came here." He said making direct eye contact with her for the first time since she opened the door.

"Well it's not home cooking but it is soul food." As he stepped in she saw the look of shock come across his face. Most people were amazed at the way the inside of her apartment looked. Her inner person was an interior decorator so she made sure that her apartment looked like it was right out of a magazine. Her living room was done in forest Green and cream. Her cream leather living room set looked awesome sitting on her forest green carpet which ran wall to wall throughout the living room. She had a beautiful glass and wood wall unit that was fully equipped with a 32" flat screen TV, DVD and stereo system that was all connected to surround sound speakers that hung from the walls. She had three matching end tables that held two lamps that matched the green in her carpet.

"You have a beautiful place." He said admiring her apartment.

"Thank you. Have a seat, I just popped in a movie. I was about to watch it since I just put my daughter to sleep." She said as she headed to the kitchen to prepare him a Tupperware full of food. As she watched him from her kitchen she saw him getting comfortable watching the movie. Thus, she took her time preparing the food. Once she was done she got two beers out the refrigerator went to the living room and handed him one.

"I don't want to be a bother." He said handing the beer back to her.

"It would bother me if you didn't drink it. I mean I already opened it." She said taking a seat next to him.

"Thanks, seriously thanks. I haven't been able to make many genuine friends here and it's nice to know everybody in this town ain't out for what you can do for them." He said staring at her with those beautiful eyes. She was almost tempted to kiss him. Almost.

...Summer

By the time Summer got home the hurt and crying had evolved into anger. Entering the house and noticing that David wasn't home only added fuel to the fire. This meant that after he left her at the restaurant he hadn't returned home. Checking their credit card statements for the time frame that he had been away she saw he had charged close to $5,000 on those two trips alone. She ran upstairs to her bedroom and started to violently throw his shit into suitcases and garbage bags. As she ripped his suits from their hangers she couldn't get those damn pictures out of her head. This time her tears represented tears of anger. All the years she invested and he just threw it down the drain for a whore. The more she packed the angrier she grew. She cursed the day she met him as she tossed one of the bags down the stairs, watching as its contents fell out on the way down. She laughed hysterically as she stomped down the stairs, putting foot prints on his highly priced silk shirts that he loved and cherished so much. As she landed at the bottom of the stairs an idea came to her as to how she would fix his ass.

She headed to the garage, got a can of spray paint, oil, and a pair of garden scissors. She headed to the kitchen, and got the bleach and marched straight into his prized living room. As she stood there a red and black spray can in each hand, her chest heaved up and down to accommodate her heavy breathing during her fit of rage. She sprayed the words WHORE LOVER all over his custom furniture. She then took the bleach and poured it all over the cushions seats. Next, she took the gasoline and poured it all over the $2,000 cream carpet. She took the scissors and stabbed the sofa up. As the cotton went flying everywhere she collapsed to the floor in tears. What had happened to her life? The one she thought was so perfect, the one she thought would flourish in happiness? It seemed as if it had all been taken away overnight. She stopped crying long enough to look at the damage she just caused and knew she had better get the hell out of there before David got home. She got up, grabbed the pictures from her bag and spread the set of them making out on the beach all over the living room. Next she wrote a note and left it on the refrigerator:

David, when I get home I want you out. I've had Frog set up a couple of bodyguards from the club to escort me home. If you are not gone by the time I return, may God be with you.

The next thing she had to do was call Frog and see if he could really hook her up with security just in case David tried to call her bluff.

As she left Frog a message on his cell phone she realized she had no place to go. She decided to head to Brooklyn to see Renee. When she reached Renee's building she was fortunate that somebody was coming out because she didn't remember her bell # and had left her cell phone in the car two blocks away. She checked the mailboxes for Renee's name, found her apartment and headed up on the elevator. As the doors opened on the 19th floor she was met with the sound of blaring rap music. The closer she got to Renee's door, the louder the music became. She was afraid to ring the bell thinking she may have the wrong apartment. Since Renee's name was on the door, she rung it despite her skepticism. A man she didn't know answered the door as marijuana smoke floated out the apartment, filling the hallway.

"I'm sorry I think I have the wrong apartment. I'm looking for Renee." Summer said trying to figure out what was going on.

"No, this is it. I'm Terrence, Renee's boyfriend." He said extending his hand.

"Boyfriend?" Summer asked too shocked to shake his extended hand.

"Yeah, I told that girl she needs to stop keeping me a secret. She's not here right now. If you want you can come in and wait for her." He said opening the door wider for her to enter. As Summer looked inside and saw two other strange men sitting on the couch she knew she had descended into bizarro world.

"Ah no, can you just tell her Summer stopped by." She said and quickly headed towards the elevator. As the elevator doors opened and Renee stepped out, Summer had never been more happy to see her in her whole life. All she could do was hug her and cry.

...Renee

As she exited the elevator and ran into Summer she was taken aback. It was bad enough she had to go and deal with Terrence who had just told her that he had people hanging out in her apartment. From the way Summer rushed into the elevator she knew Summer must've seen them as well. What was she doing here anyway? She had left a message on her cell phone for Summer to call her back, but she didn't expect her to show up unexpectedly at her apartment. Renee knew something must be wrong.

"Summer, what happened?" She asked trying to calm her friend down.

"I can't even say it can we..." She sniffed trying her best to get it out. "Can we just go somewhere and sit down? I need to sit down I just need." More sniffling. "I just need a friend right now."

Wow Renee thought to herself. What the hell is going on?

"Okay, let me just drop my gym bag off inside and we can go grab a bite to eat. Please just stop crying." Renee said taking her keys out of her bag. The closer she got to her apartment the tighter she gritted her teeth. She could hear the music from the elevator and she knew that fool wasn't smoking weed in her apartment. "This motherfucker must be trying to get me kicked out." She said to herself out loud forgetting Summer was with her.

"Who is Terrence?" Summer managed to ask.

Renee just shot her a look telling her now was not the time. She stuck her key in the door and as soon as she entered she was hit with the strong scent of marijuana smoke. Terrence turned to her flashing that smile that she once found so sexy. Now it made her sick to her stomach.

"Hey baby." He ran to her grabbed her bag and kissed her on the cheek. Summer sat in the chair closest to the door. Renee was so pissed that she didn't know whether to rudely kick them out or calmly tell him to leave.

"Lou, Tim, this is my girl Renee." He said proudly "This is Lou, he's like my brother. He's here visiting from VA and Tim is my artist I been telling you about." He said trying to grab her hand but she quickly pulled it away all while flashing a fake smile. If it had not been for Summer she likely would have flipped out on them but instead she said through her fake smile. "Terrence, can I see you in the bedroom please?" Not waiting for a response she headed to the back. As soon as he entered the room she exploded.

"Are you crazy or fucking insane? How dare you invite those hood ass motherfuckers in my house without my permission? Then have them smoking weed in my crib. What the fuck were you thinking? Or were you even thinking at all? I'm trying to look out for you and this is the thanks I get?" She said as loud as she could without the people in the front hearing.

"First of all you need to watch who the fuck you're talking to because I'm a grown ass man and not a fucking child. Second, I told you on the phone that they were on their way over. If you had a problem you should've said something then. Don't try and get all fucking cute because your little home girl is here. And I know you've been trying to keep me a secret. She ain't know who the fuck I was. I don't get that shit. If you're so fucking embarrassed by me then why the fuck you with me? I ain't no charity case. If you don't want to be bothered then say so." He said not caring who heard him.

"Why would you smoke weed in my house Terrence?" She said in a calmer tone.

"I wasn't smoking weed, they were. Yeah it was wrong but that's what they do. If I knew it would be such a fucking problem I wouldn't have let them do it. Damn, how the fuck was I suppose to know you were going to flip out over some weed. Just two weeks ago we was in bed smoking a joint." He said a little too loud for her taste.

"That was different." She said embarrassed.

"Different how Renee?" He said bringing down the bass in his voice.

"Look I'm about to step out and deal with my friend and whatever she's going through. When I get back I don't expect to find your friends here."

Instead of responding he grabbed her in his arms and started kissing on her neck and whispering in her ear. "Why you wanna make me upset with you? You know I love you."

She could not believe he just tried to throw the 'I love you' game at her. As he hugged her he started to grind himself on her letting her feel his erect penis. She pushed him away as she was surprisingly not in the mood.

"Stop we have people in the other room."

"That's what makes it more exciting." He said still trying to get at her.

"Please Terrence, stop." And he did.

"Yo, I didn't mean to disrespect you or your place. I'll make sure when you get back they're gone." He said as he slapped her on the behind heading out of the bedroom. Ten minutes later she and Summer were in Summer's car headed to who knows where.

...Constance

As Constance sat watching the movie with one eye on the television and one eye on Derrick the ringing of the telephone scared her. She excused herself, went to the kitchen and answered it thinking this better be important. *"Hello."* She answered annoyed at whoever was calling. *"Connie its Renee I hope you're not busy because if you are get unbusy."* How the hell did Renee get her new number? Then she remembered the girl worked for the telephone company. *"What's the problem?"* she asked uninterested.

"It's Summer girl. I'm with her and she needs us." Renee said.

"Summer, what happened to her?" she asked with a quiver in her voice.

"She doesn't want me to discuss it over the phone. We're on our way over to you now, we'll tell you then. We just wanted to make sure you were home." She spoke as if their argument never happened. *"You weren't busy were you?"*

"No, I wasn't busy." She said as her heart sank watching Derrick finish up his food.

"Even if I was if my girl is having a problem then I have a problem. I'll see yall when you get here." She hung up.

As she headed back to the living room she watched Derrick's moves. He must've heard part of her conversation because he stood up and handed her the plate.

"Is everything okay?" He asked.

"Yeah, I hope so." She tried to smile as she took the plate from him.

"Do you need anything?" He asked touching her shoulder making her heart skip a beat. *Damn what's happening to me?*

123

"No, I'll be fine. It's just one of my friends is going through something. Actually she's my best friend that's why I'm a little shaken up. But thanks." She said as she smelled the cologne he was wearing that was driving her crazy.

"Well if you end up needing me I'm right next door." He said smiling at her trying to make her feel better. Just knowing somebody cared made her feel better, so she returned the smile.

"Thank you Derrick, really." She said as an awkward moment arose between the two of them. He must've felt it too because he grabbed her in his arms and gave her a tight bear hug.

"Don't forget I'm a knock away." He said as he let her go and saw his way out.

Constance kept herself busy by cleaning the house until they arrived. When she opened the door she knew it was serious because Summer's eyes were blood shot and swollen as if she had been crying. Seeing her in this state startled Constance without even knowing what happened. This is how she was when it came to Summer.

...Summer

As she saw the look come across Constance's face she knew she still had tell tale signs of crying all over her face. If this is how she reacted to seeing her cry Summer could only imagine how she was going to react when she told her what was going on.

"Summer, what happened?" Constance asked.

"Do you have anything to drink up in here?" Renee asked headed toward the kitchen.

"Yeah, there's a bottle of Mo in the fridge." Constance said still looking at Summer. "Are you going to tell me what happened?"

"Well you were right about David having an affair." She said as the words spilled out of her mouth.

"Okay and you know this because?" She could see Constance had no idea what was going on so she went in her bag and handed her the photos. As she reviewed the pictures the look of confusion turned to shock.

"No." Constance said as she shook her head no. Summer shook her head indicating that it was in fact true.

"No, no, no, no don't tell me all this time that David has been fucking Honey?" Constance said with pure disgust.

"Yes. All this time that bitch has been coming to my shop, getting her hair done so she could look good for my fucking husband." Summer said taking the glass Renee handed her.

"Just like a whore." Renee said, sitting down next to Summer. Summer kept her eyes on Constance, who now paced the floor trying to understand what was going on.

"So wait. You mean to tell me when that bitch would talk about some dude she was falling for, it was David?" Constance said with anger.

"I would assume so Connie." Summer simply replied.

"I can't believe this. We going to get that bitch, tonight." She said meaning every word.

"What you talking about girl?" Renee asked.

"Exactly what I said. That bitch must be crazy if she think she's going to just get away with this. It's Sunday so you know the hoe is down at the club shaking her nasty ass for money." Constance said not caring for their approval.

"Connie we can't just go down there and beat the bitch down. She'll press charges." Renee said drinking her drink.

"She's right Connie." Summer added.

"So what, you just want her to get away with that shit?" Constance said getting upset. "If that's the case why'd you even tell me? What does David have to say about all of this?" She yelled forgetting her daughter was in the room sleep.

"Oh, that's the best part. Please can I tell this part?" Renee asked childishly. Summer just shook her head yes. She knew there was no way she would be able to tell the story again without breaking down. She just wished this would all go away like a bad dream. But as she watched Renee tell her story she knew it wouldn't.

"She destroyed the 'museum room'." Renee said excitedly.

"Destroyed it, destroyed it how?" Constance asked looking at Summer.

"She spray painted Whore Lover on the furniture, poured oil all over the rug and cut up the Sammy Davis jr. set." Renee said laughing,

"You didn't. What did he say?" Constance asked Summer.

"He wasn't there. He's been calling my cell non stop for the past hour but I haven't answered it." She said putting her head in her hands.

"What are you going to do?" Constance asked.

As she looked up at Constance she honestly didn't know what she was going to do next.

...*Renee*

As she sat there watching her friend in pain it came to her what she should do. "I've got it." She said pointing her finger in the air.

"You've got what? Constance asked looking at her.

"I know how we can get that bitch." She said standing up as all their attention focused on her next words.

"First we'll go down to the club, bust all the windows in her car, flatten her tires, and bounce. After she speaks to David she'll know it was us. That will make her come to the shop to confront us and then we'll beat her ass. Since it'll be on your property, it'll be self defense." Renee said like she just found the cure for cancer. The girls sat motionless.

"That's so stupid it just might work." Constance said smiling.

"What's stupid about it, because you didn't think of it first?" Renee said defensively.

"Girl please, it's a good idea, stop being so damn defensive." Constance said putting her glass in the sink.

"Well I don't think it's a good idea." Summer said. Renee looked at her like she was losing her mind.

"Summer please, save the good girl act okay." Renee said rolling her eyes.

"Why do you think we should let this ride?" Constance said sitting down in the arm chair. Renee watched her noticing that she had lost a couple of pounds.

"I don't know. I just don't want to make a bad situation worse." She said in a low tone. Before Renee could respond Summer answered her cell phone.

"Hello."

"Yeah this is Frog Summer what's up?"

"Hey Frog thanks for calling back." She perked up a bit.

Renee ears were at attention and her hands started to shake at the mere mention of Frog's name. She hadn't seen or spoken to him in weeks and hearing his name sent something through her that she thought was gone.

"No problem everything okay?"

"Well, no the reason I called you is I'm having a bit of a martial problem and I was wondering if you could speak to one of the body guards down at the club to escort me home tonight."

"Damn ma, sorry to hear that. Its that serious?"

"Not really but I would rather be safe than sorry you know."

"Where are you now?"

"I'm at Connie's house."

"That's perfect, one of my home boys lives next door. I'll call him and have him take you. Let me call you back, a'ight?"

"Thanks Frog." When she hung up Renee just stared at her. She wanted to say something but didn't want to say the wrong thing.

"Why didn't you tell me you needed somebody to assist you home?"

"Why would I tell you that? You're bad but you can't take on no man." She answered. Renee stayed calm as she spoke not wanting to reveal her disapproval of Summer calling Frog without her permission.

"No duh, but I would've had Terrence take you home." She said with a smile.

"Terrence? I know you didn't think I would let some guy you've been too embarrassed to even mention escort me home." She gave Renee a you've gotta be kidding me look which only made Renee more upset.

"First of all I wasn't embarrassed. I haven't really seen you since I've been seeing him, that's why I didn't mention it. And I think it's a little rude for you to be calling Sean for anything." She said not caring anymore.

"Rude? Renee what's rude about it? Do you think I need your permission to call Frog?" She asked as Renee saw the anger developing in her eyes.

"No I don't think you need my permission but he is my ex and you shouldn't be communicating with him at all."

"Look enough with this nonsense. Are we going down to the club or not?"

Constance said changing the subject.

"I'm going." Renee said not thinking twice about it.

"Well Frog is supposed to be calling me back to see if your next door neighbor will take me home." Summer said looking at Constance.

...Constance

Now why she had to go there? How dare she try and get Derrick involved with this mess. "Why are you trying to get innocent people involved in this when you don't even want to go down to the club and handle your business?" Constance said speaking before she could stop herself.

"Whose side are you two on?" Summer asked.

"You know I'm on yours." And she meant that she didn't know what got into her. "Look you stay here because Meagan is in the room asleep. Renee and I will go down to the club. Don't leave until we get back."

"How could I leave when Meagan is here?" Summer replied.

"You ready?" Renee asked slipping her shoes back onto her feet.

"Yeah, let's go. We'll take my car."

They drove to the club and circled the block as Connie wondered if Honey even worked at the club anymore. She had remembered one of the clients saying they hadn't seen her in a while.

"Isn't that her car right there?" Renee asked pointing to a Champagne colored Lexus. Constance knew it was hers because of the vanity license plate that read HUNYLUV.

"Yep that's it. You ready?" She asked Renee.

"Yeah I'm ready. Good thing she didn't park in an open area." Constance said double parking a car behind Honey's." She popped the trunk and removed her crow bar. She handed Renee a tool so she could bust the tires while she broke the windows.

"How do you want to do this?" Renee asked Constance as they got out the car.

"First you flatten the tires then I'll bust the windows." As she said it her adrenaline began to pump. All the pain she had watched Summer go through only fueled her more.

"Do you really think this'll work?" Renee asked looking as if she were having second thought. Constance seeing the uneasiness in her eyes said.

"Why shouldn't it? It's was your idea." She watched as the smile crept across Renee's face.

"You're right." And with that she went and flattened the tires. After she was done with the Fourth one she took the hammer and busted the driver side window. "Bitch."

"Hey, I'm supposed to bust the windows." Constance smiled to herself thinking *this bitch done lost her mind.*

"Sorry." Renee said holding her head to the side as she took the hammer and put it through the windshield. After Constance broke the remaining windows they jumped in the car and drove off like they were never there.

As they sat at a red light she knew she heard her but wasn't sure.

"Connie did you hear me? Isn't that Reggie over there?"

...Renee

No she didn't just run the damn light? "Connie what is wrong with you? I can't believe you just ran the light. I wish you would slow down. You act like we're running from the law." Renee looked at her wondering what just happened. As she watched the color slowly come back to Constance's face she wondered what that was all about. Why did she panic at the sight of Reggie?

"Connie, is everything all right?"

"Do you think he saw us?" She asked checking her rearview mirror to make sure they weren't being followed.

"No I don't think so. Why are you running from Reggie?" Renee asked looking at her like she had just lost her mind.

"It's a long story." The further away they got the calmer she became. Renee made a mental note to ask Summer if she knew anything about what had just happened.

"I haven't seen Sean since the Fourth of July." Renee said looking down at her hands. Despite her new fix, she was starting to miss him. She shook it off as a feeling she was having because Summer had spoke of him earlier today.

"I know. He told me the last time I spoke to him. I'm sorry if I had anything to do with it." Connie said sincerely . Renee knew what she said was genuine.

"It's cool. I guess it was going to happen sooner or later. When did you see him?" She asked trying to get some information.

"It must've been a week or two ago, I ran into him while he was visiting Derrick." Connie said keeping her eye on the road.

"What made him bring my name up?" Renee asked thinking maybe he missed her too.

"Actually I brought your name up. I had asked him how you were doing and that's when he told me he hadn't spoken to you since the Fourth." She said glancing over at Renee as she drove.

"Did he say anything else?" Renee watched Connie as she started to develop a smirk on her face.

"Why, you miss him?"

"Just answer the damn question Connie." Renee said with a giggle.

"Well, he said he heard you were messing around with some drug dealer from VA." Constance said as she looked at Renee with a 'is that true' look.

Drug dealer? What the fuck are they talking about?

"Drug dealer? Who told him Terrence was a drug dealer? He's not a drug dealer, he's a producer. He's here producing an album for some kid. I even met the boy tonight before we came over to your house." Renee said defensively.

"Don't shoot the messenger." Connie said holding her hand up. "I'm just telling you what the man said." She put her hands back on the wheel and left Renee in her own thoughts.

I have to figure out what's going on. Where would Sean get the idea that Terrence is dealing drugs? Is he dealing drugs and just telling me he's a producer? Is that why I found that coke in his pockets? But if he was a drug dealer why isn't he bringing in No Money? I don't want Sean thinking I'm fucking with drug dealers. He should know me better than that. I gotta talk to him.

...David

As he drove away from the restaurant he knew Summer would hit the roof when she discovered that he had left her, but he didn't care anymore. Things were getting out of hand and starting to fall apart. He didn't know what to say to her about the statement. He had forgotten all about the monthly statement because he hadn't seen one in years. Summer was the one who handled all of their finances. He had to get away and think about what to do. It was bad enough Honey had called Summer when they were away and he had to explain that. He knew his wife didn't believe him especially since she had Constance in her ear pointing out all the lies and discrepancies.

At first he was going to call Honey and have her meet him somewhere but he knew that wouldn't be such a wise idea since he was trying to end it with her. She was becoming too attached and he had to make a move. He knew once she called his wife it had to end. What was she trying to prove? He had lost count of the number of times she had asked him when he was going to leave Summer. He would wonder to himself *when the fuck did I ever say I was leaving my wife?* Yes they were having trouble getting pregnant but he truly loved her with all his heart. He had first started seeing Honey because he felt helpless in pleasing his wife. A baby was the one thing she wanted more than anything and he couldn't do anything to provide it. He had purchased the shop for her to help her ease the pain but that only helped for a while. She was back at it again and he was getting tired of it. He just wished she would either leave it alone or adopt. But adopting wasn't even an option in her book.

He had met Honey one night after he had stayed out late with a co-worker drinking. He had lost track of time and when he got home Summer was crying and screaming. He tried to explain to her that he had simply lost track of time but she just wouldn't let it die. He figured Constance must've started putting thoughts in her head because this wasn't his wife standing in front of him yelling like this. It was out of character. Once she started throwing things at him he tried to walk out the room but she wouldn't let up. She ran behind him grabbing on his shirt pulling him back and before he knew it, he turned around and slapped her. As soon as he did, he knew things would never be the same. "I'm so sorry." He said as he went to try and help her up.

"Don't touch me!" She yelled as he saw the look of fear in her eyes. His heart felt cold as the pain eased up and was caught in his throat. He had never wanted to see that look on his wife's face. He had seen that look time and time again in his mother's eyes as his father would come home and put his hands on her.

"Summer, please, you know I didn't mean to hit you." He sat on the floor next to her trying to console her but she wouldn't let him.

"Just leave, please. Just leave me alone." She begged through tears. And that's what he did. Due to the fact it was so late a lot of places were closed. Eventually he found his way to the local strip bar to get a drink and to calm down.

"Hey baby, you want a lap dance?" He really didn't. He wasn't there for the women. He was there to clear his head but figured what the heck and that was the beginning of their love affair. The affair that he knew had brought his marriage to an end. It had gotten out of hand and now that Summer was starting to put two and two together he wanted nothing to do with Honey. He had left the restaurant to go and find Honey and let her know it was over. He had tried to tell her on the trip to Florida but she acted as if she didn't want to hear it. As he headed to her apartment he tried to figure out the best way to end it. As he rung her doorbell he still hadn't come up with the best way to put it. She answered the door in a red teddy and he rolled his eyes at her attempt to try and change his mind. He called her to let her know he was on his way to talk. Why she would answer the door half naked was beyond him.

"What's your problem?" She said closing the door.

"Why don't you put some clothes on?" He said looking at her with disgust.

"Why, am I tempting you to do something you don't want to?" She said rubbing her hands on his chest. He pushed her away and sat down in the arm chair.

"It really doesn't matter what you wear. I came over here to tell you this shit is over." He said looking in her eyes letting her know he was serious.

"Why, is Summer pregnant?" She said laughing.

He felt like slapping her. She knew better than to talk about his wife like that. Shit, she knew better than to mention her name at all.

"What goes on under my roof is none of your business. I said it's over and that's it. Don't you ever let my wife's name come out of your mouth again. You understand me?" He said angrily.

"Oh please David. If she isn't pregnant the drama will continue and you will still need somebody to make you happy." She said kneeling in front of him.

"Well that's something I'll have to deal with, not you. So don't worry about it." He said getting up from the chair.

"You can't do this to me." She said standing up hugging him and pressing her fake breasts up against him.

"Honey, come on now. You knew this wasn't going to last so cut it out." He said heading for the door. "If you leave me I'll tell her everything." She said as he stopped and turned to face her.

"She already knows." He said not conceding to her threat. "Maybe, but I bet she doesn't know it's with me." She said twisting her lips.

"What difference does that make? An affair is an affair. You think she cares about who it's with?"

"That's what you think. Who do you think does my hair? Haven't you ever wondered why when she went on her hair convention why I wasn't around either?" She said looking at him with a devilish smirk on her face. He was so upset he chose not to respond.

"Make sure you lose my number." And he left.

As he drove home his mind was everywhere. He only hoped that this wouldn't get as big as he knew it could. When he entered the house and saw clothes all over the place his heart started to pound. His first thought was someone broke in the house. As he called out Summer's name it was apparent that she was not home. When he saw the mess in the room and what she had done to the furniture he knew things had already gotten out of hand. What confused him were the pictures all over the floor of him and Honey. *Where the hell did she get these from?*

As upset as he was about her tearing up the furniture and destroying the room he could understand where the anger was coming from. He headed to the bathroom where he kept his secret stash and tried his best to make his troubles go away.

...Summer

By the time Constance and Renee got back Summer had fallen asleep on the couch. She spoke to Frog and he informed her that he was on his way over so he and Derrick could take her home. As they woke her up she was happy they got back before Frog got there.

"So what happened?" She asked sitting up on the couch.

"It went the way it was supposed to go." Constance said putting their weapons of destruction away.

"I'm going to make a drink. Anybody want one?" Renee asked as she headed to the kitchen to finish off the Moet.

"Not me." Summer said. She was beginning to feel nauseous. "Don't you think you're starting to drink too much."

"I'm grown, so no, I don't think so. I only drink on the weekends anyway so what are you talking about?" Renee asked. Summer ignored her defense.

"Do you think she'll come by the shop?" She asked Constance.

"Only time will tell." She said taking her drink from Renee. "Did Derrick stop by?"

"No, but Frog called and said he was on his way. I guess he'll stop by Derrick's and then come and get me." She said headed to the bathroom to relieve herself of the nausea. When she returned Constance was giving her a funny look.

"What's up with that?" Constance asked.

"I guess the liquor got to me." She answered sitting back down.

"Liquor? You had one glass and that was hours ago." Constance pressed.

"She's right you know." Renee said adding her two cents.

"So." Summer replied not understanding where they were trying to go.

"Maybe you're pregnant." Constance said smiling.

"You do look like you've put on a couple of pounds." Renee said.

"Yeah right. It's called stress. Stress makes you eat more and that's what I've been doing." Summer said ignoring their stares.

"When was your last period?" Constance asked refusing to drop the topic.

"Look, from the hormone shots I take my period acts up so even if I was pregnant I couldn't go by my cycle." She said wishing they would just drop it.

"Just answer the question. When was your last period?" Constance asked again.

"I don't know three months ago." Summer replied rolling her eyes.

"When was your last doctor's visit?" Renee questioned.

"Around the same time." Summer said as Constance's buzzer went off. Summer was happy because this was something she wasn't comfortable talking about because of the sensitivity of the topic.

"That must be Frog." Constance said as she buzzed the door.

"Shouldn't you have at least asked first?" Renee said headed to the kitchen to fix herself another drink. Her nerves were starting to play around in her stomach.

...Renee

As soon as he stepped inside of the apartment she knew she still loved him. Seeing him again set her heart on fire and it showed all over her face. When he walked in smiling Renee almost went over and kissed him but controlled her inner urge and just said. "Hi."

"Wow. It feels good in here. It is mad muggy out there." He said fanning his shirt. She watched him as he greeted Summer and Constance with kisses to the check and as he headed her way she kept telling herself 'be cool'. When he leaned in to kiss her the first thing that hit her was his scent. He was still wearing the cologne she brought him and this made her smile inside.

"So how you been?" He asked her.

"I'm cool." She replied smiling.

"Good. It's nice to know you're doing alright." He said turning to Summer.

"So you ready to head home? I have someplace I should've been a ½ hour ago."

"Date?" Renee said instinctually.

"Excuse me?" He said turning to her knowing fully well he heard her.

"Nothing. It's just you're all dressed up." She said admiring his cream linen Sean John short set. His braids were shining and freshly done. On his feet he wore a pair of black Steve Madden sandals.

"Okay. Summer, you ready?" He turned back to Summer ignoring Renee's line of questioning. This made her upset and as bad as she wanted to put him in his place she held her tongue. She knew he must still be hurting over what happened. The fact that he knew she had already moved on didn't help matters any.

"Yeah, I'm ready whenever you are." Summer answered.

"Let's go then. Derrick is downstairs in the car. Which reminds me, he told me to tell you hi." He said looking at Constance. Renee noticed the smile creep across her face at the mere mention of Derrick's name. This brought her back to earlier with the Reggie incident. Something was definitely up.

"Tell him I said hey." She said blushing.

"Yeah, I'll talk to you about that later." Frog said as he opened the door. "Wait I'm going out too. I have to work in the morning." Renee said grabbing her bag. "That is of course if you don't mind dropping me off Sean. I came in Summer's car." If he agreed she could try and get to the bottom of this drug dealer talk.

"Renee, I told you I have to be somewhere. How about if I give you cab fare?" He said as they headed downstairs.

"Well there are a few things we need to discuss and I thought this would be the best time if any." She said pressing the issue.

"Things like what?" He asked sounding annoyed.

"Like your attitude for starters." She answered.

"Fine Renee, whatever." He said giving in as they exited the building.

...Summer

As they pulled up in her driveway she couldn't help but wonder if she had made a mistake by getting all these people involved in her marital problems. Seeing David's car in the driveway only sent her nervous system to overdrive. She wished that he had taken her message serious and just left.

"Is that his car?" Frog asked her.

"Yep." She responded.

"Let's go then." He said getting out of the car. Summer said a silent prayer that everything would go smoothly. As she walked in the door with Frog, Derrick and Renee in tow the first thing that caught her eye was a vase in the kitchen that was broken on the floor with flowers and water surrounding it. Her heart began to race as her mind began to wonder. "Why is that door open?" she said to no one in particular referring to the back door that led to the yard.

"That's a good question." She heard Derrick reply.

"David!" She called out his name. "David!" She called again.

"Maybe he's not here. Let's just leave." She heard Renee say as her voice quivered.

"His car is outside. Where else would he be?" Summer asked.

"Maybe he went to the store." Renee replied.

"The store is 10 blocks away, he would've taken his car." Summer said as she walked through the house. As she was about to head upstairs she heard Renee screaming.

"Ahhhhhhhhhh!"

She ran to see what happened and that's when she saw it. Her husband lay motionless in a pool of blood inside the family room. She was too shocked to move. She felt Frog push her out of the way as he ran over and checked David's pulse.

"Call 911, he's still breathing." He yelled at her. She remained in shock. Derrick pulled out his cell phone and called 911.

As the doctors questioned her she just shook her head in response to their questions and said nothing. Renee had gone in Summer's purse and given them all the insurance information that they requested. Next, the NYPD questioned her while Frog sat with her and helped her answer their questions the best they could. Since they arrived after the shooting there wasn't much information they could provide to help with the investigation. After the cops left they sat in the waiting area for the doctors to tell them David's prognosis.

"Do you think it was a robbery?" Frog asked her.

Not knowing how to answer she shrugged her shoulders.

"It didn't look like a robbery to me." Derrick added. "Aside from the mess that you guys said Summer did, everything looked fine."

"Summer, do you have any idea who would do this?" Frog asked her. She wished he would stop questioning her. Wasn't he right there when she told the cops she had no idea what happened. After two hours, a doctor finally emerged and told her she could go in and see her husband.

As she made her way inside of the room the tears in her eyes clouded her vision and she couldn't make out which bed he laid in. Pulling herself together she was able to make him out. He was still drugged and semi conscious as she made her way to his bed and grabbed his hand.

"David, can you hear me?" She said with a shaky voice. He looked at her and squeezed her hand. He had been shot two times, once in the shoulder, and once in the leg. She leaned over and kissed him on his lips which were now dry and chapped.

"Baby, you're going to be okay." The tears made their way down her cheek.

"I can't stay long, but I'll be back tomorrow okay?" He tried to smile and that made her feel a little better. He was trying to say something but she couldn't make it out because he kept slipping in and out of consciousness.

"Don't try and talk David, save your energy." He tried anyway and she was finally able to make out the words "I'm sorry."

"I'll see you tomorrow." She said as she got prepared to leave. Until now she had forgotten all about him having the affair. At this point that was no longer a priority.

...Renee

After they dropped Summer off at Constance's house Renee finally had time to talk to Sean alone. She wasn't sure if she should even bring up her problem with all the drama that went down tonight. The thought that kept going through her head was if them busting out Honey's windows had anything to do with David being shot. She convinced herself that this was impossible and quickly let the feeling go. Just as she was about to ask Sean about his conversation with Connie regarding Terrence his phone rang. He answered it on speaker phone. Once the female voice emerged on the other end he looked at Renee and picked the phone up.

"Damn, I'm so sorry, forgive me. A friend of mine ran into an emergency and I couldn't get out of it." She heard him say.

"Well you could've at least called."

"I know but I didn't have time to call and to be honest I've been so consumed with what happened it slipped my mind. I promise you I'll make it up." Who is he talking to she wondered.

"Hello!! This was a make up date."

"I know." He seems to care about whomever it is Renee thought.

"Look, call me when you can keep a promise and not before."

As he hung up the phone she couldn't help but feel jealous.

"So you did have a date tonight?" She asked him snooping.

"What do you care about what I'm doing? Aren't you seeing somebody?"

He asked sounding upset. Perfect, she thought, here's my chance.

"Well nothing serious, but I'm glad you brought that up. Constance told me you said he was a drug dealer. Where'd you get that from?"

"I don't know. Somebody told me they saw you in some club with him and they said he was a drug dealer to people in the industry." He said looking at her.

"He's a producer not a drug dealer." She said defensively.

"Whatever, I hope you're happy." He said in a dismissive tone.

"Actually, I was happy with you." She said.

"Yeah, well you seem to have moved on pretty fast." He replied glancing at her.

"Me? You don't seem to be doing so bad your damn self." Renee said folding her arms.

"Yeah, sit there with your arms folded like a spoiled baby. I loved you Renee, for whatever reason you weren't able to see that so you chose to move on. Don't sit here and try and act like I was supposed to sit around and wait for you to realize that." He said raising his voice.

"I've always known that and you know it. Just like you know I loved you back, I still love you." She said matter of factly.

"You love me?" He said with a chuckle. "Is that why you're out running around town with your new boyfriend. Got niggas coming up to me telling me about seeing out with this dude. Does *he* know you still love me Renee?"

"I'm only with him to pass the time while I get over losing you." She said so low he almost didn't hear her.

"Well I hope it's time well spent." He said shaking his head as he focused on the road.

"Do you hate me?" She asked him.

"Renee, what's up with you? I gave you everything and it still wasn't enough. You're forgetting that you're the one who said that they wanted space. Shit, after what happened in your office that day I should've been the one wanting space from you. So don't sit here questioning me about my love for you. You need to wake up and ask yourself do *you* hate you?"

"You're right Sean. I made a huge mistake and if given a second chance I would take it all back without a second thought." She said as she looked at him pleading for forgiveness.

"That's funny Renee because you don't seem like somebody who wants a second chance. Before I could even digest what happened you was telling me you wanted space. Next thing I know somebody's occupying that space." He said glancing at his watch, a clear sign that he didn't have time for this.

"Well goodnight, thanks for the ride." As she got out of the car she knew she had lost him. She slowly walked back to her building feeling him watching her as she made it in safely. He beeped his horn calling her back.

"Yeah?" She said not trying to hide the hurt she felt. She was tired of hiding the way she felt for him.

"I'm on my last bottle of cologne so if you don't mind could you get me some more? That is of course if homeboy ain't getting it now." He said with less attitude in his voice.

"Don't be silly, you know I got you." She said with a smile.

"Goodnight Renee." He said smiling back.

As Renee slept that night for the first time in a long time she had a warm feeling inside as she drifted off to sleep thinking maybe she still had a chance.

...Constance

As Constance watched Summer sleep she wondered how they had gotten to this point. She could remember a time when they didn't have a care in the world. Now here she was watching her friend sleep as she thought about all the shit that had gone down. Her husband shot, Reggie; what happened to them? Her mind drifted to the movie that sat in her closet. She hadn't watched it since leaving the hotel that night, but for some reason it was calling her name. She figured it was because she had saw Reggie for the first time since that fateful discovery.

She went into her closet, into the box where she left the tape and got it out. Not wanting to wake Summer or Meagan she took it into the living room, put it in the player and hit play. When the video started she could see the woman in the bathroom as he got everything situated. Fifteen minutes later he was wining and dining her. He didn't wine and dine me. She thought as the tears stung her eyes. She watched as he slowly undressed the woman making her perform a little dance for him. She couldn't help but notice how much he was enjoying it all. She didn't realize how hard she was crying until Summer said her name.

"Constance what's going on?" Summer asked.

Surprised by Summer's presence she shuffled with the remote trying to stop the tape, but by the time she found the stop button she knew it was too late.

"Summer, what are you doing up?" Constance asked as she wiped the tears.

"Connie what is going on?" Summer asked again ignoring her question. Knowing she couldn't keep lying to her friend she decided to come clean.

"I want to tell you Summer but you're going through so much right now."

She managed to say through tears.

"Constance I'm going to ask you one more time, what is going on?" Summer asked as she walked over to console her friend.

Knowing that she couldn't keep this to herself any longer, she decided to confide in her friend.

"After you left me on the Fourth I found this video in the apartment. It's one of many videos that Reggie made of women that he slept with in that loft and I'm on it too." She said as the thought brought more tears.

"And you've been keeping this from me all this time?" Summer said.

"I was embarrassed Summer. Can't you understand that? I was violated in the worst way by somebody I thought I loved. I found out in the worst way that he's been violating other women too. This woman on the tape is the same one he told me was a client of his." She said as she placed her head in her hands.

"I'm sorry Constance." Summer said as she rubbed her friends back. "I had no idea Reggie was such an ass."

"How could you, I didn't even know." She sobbed.

"What do you plan on doing?" Summer asked.

"What can I do? There's nothing I can do." She said getting up.

"You must be crazy, I'm sure this is illegal. He taped you without your permission. He probably didn't have any of these women's permission."

Summer said getting upset.

"You really think I can do something?" Constance asked, wiping her tears away.

"Let me put it like this. If we can't we'll just send the tape to his wife, either way he ain't getting away with this shit." Summer said meaning every word.

"When did you become so evil?" Constance asked showing a hint of a smile

"When my sister got fucked with." Summer added smiling back.

...*Summer*

As she rose the next morning the first thing she did was head to the bathroom to throw up. For the first time she wondered if she was in fact pregnant. She had asked Connie to go to the shop and open up for her because she wanted to go to the hospital to check up on David.

As she headed to the hospital so many thoughts were going through her head. Now that her husband was laying in the hospital shot should she still divorce him? Could she ever reconcile with David after seeing those pictures and that tape? Who could've shot him? Was he shot because they busted out Honey's car windows? She wasn't planning to talk to him about it now because he was still recovering. She just hoped that he had some answers today as to what happened the night before. She was too shaken up to go to the house last night. But she knew she would have to return home sooner or later. As she approached his hospital room she said a silent prayer that everything would work itself out.

When she entered his room she was happy he had been moved to the recovery unit. The ICU was just too intense for her. As she watched his face light up at the sight of her entering his room, it warmed her heart. At that moment she knew she could find a way to work through this.

"Hey Pumpkin." He said through a whisper.

"Hi." She said as she went over and gave him a kiss before sitting in the chair next to his bed.

"I'm glad you're here Summer." He said with sorrow in his eyes.

"I'm your wife David, where else would I be?" She replied grabbing his hand, a clear indication that she was going to stick it through with him.

"Summer, I'm sorry. Please know that I never meant to hurt you." He said as she saw the tears build in his eyes.

"David, we have plenty of time to deal with that. Right now you need to focus on getting back on your feet." She said caressing his hands.

"I love you." He said pulling her hand up to his lips.

"I know you do." She said smiling at him.

"Have you spoken to the cops today?" He asked her.

"No, should I have?" She asked surprised by the question.

"No, I just thought they would've filled you in on what I told them." He said.

"What happened David?" She asked him while adjusting his pillow.

"Well after I left you at the restaurant I drove around trying to figure out how I got myself involved in this mess. So I drove over to her house."

Her. Don't you mean Honey.

"Well when I got there of course she wasn't happy with the choice I made. So she acted out a bit." He said trying his best not to look her in the eye.

"What made you want to end it? Because you got caught?" Summer asked trying her best not to get upset.

"I just did. It had nothing to do with getting caught." He answered as he shifted nervously in the bed.

"Well did you at least get a look at the person's face?" She said as she helped him get comfortable.

"Yeah, he didn't even have enough sense to wear a mask. He kept asking where the safe was?" He said but she interrupted him.

"What safe?"

"That's what I tried to tell him. I told him there was no safe and that's when he shot me." He replied.

"Do you think he'll come back?" she asked worried that they might have to sell the house.

"I don't know but I called ADT this morning and they'll be out to the house on Wednesday. Hopefully I'll be home by then but until then I want you to stay with Connie." He said now looking her directly in the eye.

"That shouldn't be a problem. David, I have to know why you would sleep with one of my clients." Summer asked forgetting her earlier commitment to focus only on his recovery.

"It's a long story, but please believe I didn't know you knew her at all. She just told me that last night." He said as he held her hand tighter. "I love you Summer and I just didn't know how to deal with us not getting pregnant. I know that sounds like an excuse but it's the truth. I never meant for it to go this far."

"Well it did David and God only knows if it's really over."

...Renee

When Renee got home from work that Monday, she was relieved that Terrence wasn't there. Unfortunately another surprise awaited her as his 'brother' Lou was waiting outside her door. It was going close to midnight and she wasn't in the mood to entertain.

"How you doing?" He asked as she opened the door.

"Hi." She said as she let him in even though she had no intention to.

As they entered the apartment he took a seat on her couch.

"So, where's your man at?" He asked her.

"Man? Are you talking about Terrence? Because if you are I haven't seen him in the past two days. The last time I saw him he was here with you." She said as she took a seat in her chair.

"Two days huh. You sure bout that?"

"That's what I said, why?" She asked wondering why this man was at her home.

"Why?" He laughed repeating her question. "Don't you know?"

"Know what?" she asked regretting letting him in.

"Terrence owes me money. A lot of money." He said admiring his manicured nails.

"I thought you were his brother." She asked getting confused.

"Look, all that bullshit is out the window. He is cool with me as long as he can get me that paper he owes me." He said as he looked up at her.

"Well if and when I hear from him I'll let him know you're looking for him." She said as she got up to see him out. "Until then I would appreciate you not coming by my home unless you are invited by me." She unlocked the door and he stood up and lit a cigarette and flashed a fake smile.

"I like your style. I only wish that bitch ass boyfriend of yours had as much heart as you did. When you see him you tell him I want the rest of my money and I want my shit."

"I will and please don't smoke in here." She said as she opened the door for him. He blew smoke from his mouth before saying.

"You have no idea who you're involved with?"

"I guess not."

"Yeah well here's a little piece of advice. Next time be careful who you pick up in gyms." He said as he blew more smoke into her apartment.

"Yeah well I doubt there will be a next time."

"Whatever just make sure you get my message to Terrence." He said as he walked past her blowing out more smoke.

Once he was gone she didn't know what to do. She had been so desperate to move on from Sean that she picked up just anybody. Only this time he was the wrong somebody. As she went to her room to check her things to make sure nothing was missing she couldn't help but berate herself. How could she give her keys to a man she barely knew based on his sex game. She had totally lost her mind this time. She knew the only thing left to do was get his shit together and finally get his ass out of her life.

She headed straight towards her bedroom and started gathering his things from her closet. She grabbed his two duffle bags and started to fill them with his belongings. As she unzipped the second bag her eyes widened at the sight of a few thousand in cash and what seemed about a boatload of what had to be cocaine. Her heart skipped beats as her hands shook. It was more serious than she had thought. Here he was bringing drugs into her home putting her life in danger. Her first thought was to flush the drugs and money but she knew the streets better than that. She decided she would go straight to the source. She got her thoughts together and went out into the night to find Terrence. She wanted him out of her life and she wanted him out now. She went to the one place he might be at 2:00 in the morning, the studio.

...Constance

As Constance tried her best to maintain all the customers, she was shocked to see Summer walk in. It was after 1 in the afternoon and she was planning to close the shop early due to it being understaffed. When Summer walked in all her clients started clapping. They had stayed hoping that she would show and here she was in the flesh. Constance clapped on the inside because as good as she was she knew she couldn't sew a weave like Summer could. Justice was the first to speak which was only fair as she had waited for Summer since 9 am.

"Girl I'm so happy to see you I knew you wouldn't leave me hanging." She said as she jumped into Summer's chair.

"Thank you for waiting." Summer said as she prepared to do her hair.

"I'm next!" Gail said from the waiting area.

"Alright Gail don't worry. I wrote everybody down as they came in."

Constance said smiling knowing every client wasn't leaving until Summer 'hooked them up'. She couldn't blame them. Summer was one of the most sought after hair stylists this side of town. She was in many eyes the best weave hair stylist in all of NYC. Constance pulled her to the side still worried about what was going in her personal life.

"Is David okay?" She asked with concern.

"Yeah, they should be releasing him tomorrow so I'll be out of your hair."

She said with a smile.

"Don't be silly you weren't a bother to me."

"Yeah well it will be nice to sleep in my own bed again."

"I'm sure it will."

CRASH!

Constance turned just in time to see the brick that hit the window fall to the floor. All the customers jumped up screaming. A few had glass on their clothing and in their hair. "What the fuck?" Constance yelled as she raced to the door. When she got outside she saw Honey standing in front of her car with plastic in place of where her windows had once been. She was with two other strippers from the club who had also come to the shop before to get their hair done.

"Yeah bitch, where the fuck is your punk ass friend?" She said waving her hand. Summer made her way through the crowd that gathered at the door.

"Who the fuck you calling a bitch, whore? Yo Summer, go call the cops on these bitches." Constance yelled getting more upset by the minute.

"Call'em bitch. Call'em right now so I can show them what the fuck your punk ass did to my car. I should fuck your ass up right now. Don't be mad at me because your man wants this pussy." She said pointing to her genital area.

"Don't flatter yourself. You just mad he don't want it. Now take your stank ass back down to the whore house you climbed out of so you can pay your rent. And take them chickens with you." Constance yelled as Summer pulled her back inside.

"Fuck you Connie, you need to mind your business before I call your man's wife. You ain't no better than me bitch. At least I gets paid." She could hear Honey scream as Summer sat Constance in a chair.

"What you pull me in for? I should go and smack that hoe." Constance said as her blood continued to boil.

"No you shouldn't. Justice already called the cops and they are on their way. When they get here she is the only one getting arrested." Summer said trying to calm Constance down.

"Well they better hurry the fuck up."

159

"Summmmer bring your punk ass out here and fight me like a woman bitch. You was woman enough to break my windows when I wasn't looking. Be woman enough to step to my face." They heard her yelling from outside.

"What's wrong with her?" Justice asked, still shaken up from the window being broken.

"Isn't she a client? I've been in a few hair shows with her." Another client said.

"I'm getting out of here, I don't have time for this shit." She heard another say as she got her bags together.

"Precious." Summer stopped her. "I wish you would stay and give the cops your account of what happened."

"I don't think so. Summer I love you and wish you the best but I don't talk to cops. I'm sorry." She said as she hurried out the door.

"I'll stay." Justice said as a few more clients chimed in that they would stay and give a report on what happened. Simultaneously, a few more clients followed Precious out the door. As Constance sat there watching them she wondered how far this would go.

...Summer

Never did I think the chick would come and bust *my* window she thought as she stood there telling the cops her story realizing that this was getting out of control. When Honey saw the cops pull up her and her crew rolled out. But not before Constance pointed them out. One of the cop cruisers pulled her over for questioning. It was a good thing that nobody had witnessed them breaking her windows but a very good thing that so many saw her break Summer's.

"Do you want to press charges?" Summer heard one of the cops ask a client that had gotten cut by the glass.

"Yes I do." She said with attitude.

"Mrs. Johnson we are going to need you to come down to the station and fill out some paper work." The officer said to Summer.

"Sure. What about my business though? I can't just leave with the window open." She responded, wondering what she should do.

"Go ahead and handle your business. I'll call Frog, tell him what happened and have him send someone over to handle the window." Connie said sounding like the voice of reason.

"Alright, make sure you call me and let me know what happens." She said as she left with the cop.

As she drove to the police station she kept hearing the hurt and anger in Honey's voice. It was as if she blamed Summer because David ended their relationship when in fact she was the one who had help ruin her marriage. Her cell phone rang and she checked the number and saw it was David calling from the hospital. He was probably wondering why she hadn't called to say she made it back to the shop. She answered on speaker phone.

"Hello"

"Pumpkin are you okay?"

She could tell from his tone of voice he had already called the shop.

"Yes David I'm fine." She said not wanting him to worry.

"I just called the shop and Constance told me what happened."

Of course she did.

"David it's not as bad as you think. I'm fine. All she did was break the window."

"Summer! That's serious. Don't make this out to be something minor when you know it's major. This is all my fault damn, I wish I could just erase everything that's been happening." He said. She hadn't seen him this emotional since the night he hit her.

"David please calm down. We will deal with this but we have to be strong." She didn't need him breaking down now.

"That's easy for you to say. You're not the one bringing drama into our home, I am."

"David was you thinking about all this when you were out spending our money on this bitch? No! So don't sit here talking this crap to me now. I'm trying to be strong through this and not end this marriage, so I'm sure you can be strong enough to hold me down. Yes, you are the one who brought this drama into our home, but its here now. What we need to do is focus on how to get the bullshit out." She yelled as the events began to wear down her psyche.

"You're right, I'm sorry. I guess instead of focusing on the past I need to be looking toward our future." He said in a low voice. Now that they were on the same page they would be able to move past all of this mess. At least she hoped they could.

...Renee

When Renee pulled up in front of the studio she felt a chill run through her body. She couldn't stop beating herself up for leaving a good man like Sean to get involved with a loser like Terrence. She was so caught up on how good his sex was she overlooked a lot of things that she usually wouldn't. "The Studio" was in the basement of someone's home in Brownsville, Brooklyn. She had come here a few times to pick him up so she was somewhat familiar with the surroundings. The studio was home to excessive weed smoking and late night drinking that sometimes went on till 5 or 6 o'clock in the morning.

As she walked through looking for Terrence she recognized the song playing because it was one that Terrence would play over and over in the house. She even sang along to the chorus as she walked in. In one corner of the room stood a large club sized speaker with a couch next to it that looked like it had seen better days. On the couch sat a young guy in his twenties and a girl likely younger than that making out. On the opposite side of the room was a pull out couch that was being occupied by a couple having sex. Renee almost pulled the covers off of them to see exactly what they were doing but wisely decided against it. The lighting was low due to the red and green light bulbs that lit the room. As she made her way to the back of the studio there were a few guys in the hallway smoking weed and rapping. When she walked through the entrance a few stopped and looked at her.

"Hey sexy, what you need?" One asked.

"Yo that's me son." Another said grabbing himself.

She was sorry she even came inside here. Now she knew why she was only allowed to wait outside in the car.

"Do you know Terrence?" She asked sounding out of place.

"Who?" Another said moving too close for her comfort.

163

"Terrence!" She tried to yell over the loud music.

"Who the fuck is that?" The first one who spoke asked.

"Oh, you mean Tee. He's in the back." One of them answered pointing toward the back of the basement.

As she made her way to the back she couldn't help but ask herself *why don't you just change your locks?* When she got to the room where he was, any doubt she had about him was confirmed. She watched as he sat at a table with his artist Tim and two other girls. Coke, baggies and scales were all over the table. Most of it was loose, while the rest were bagged up in small and large baggies. She had never seen anything like it her whole life outside of a movie. She watched how Terrence measured the drugs with perfection as Tim and the other two girls bagged it up. Tim took the smoke from the girl that was sitting closet to him. While the other girl and Terrence snorted coke off the back of her hand. She couldn't help but notice how the two girls looked too young to be out this late without somebody looking for them. They each had on their bra with a pair of spandex, Renee figured so they couldn't steal anything. When Tim passed the blunt to Terrence, she watched how he inhaled the smoke while closing his eyes smiling. He slowly exhaled the smoke through his nose. The smell of the drugs they smoked crept up her nostrils and almost caused her to choke. She raised her hand to her face to try and prevent herself from inhaling it.

When he opened his eyes and saw Renee standing there watching him he quickly tried to pass the blunt off to one of the girls as he walked toward her.

"Hey baby, what are you doing here? You shouldn't be here."

"That's the same question I've been trying to figure out myself."

"I'm sorry I've been away for a few days but we've been crammed up in here trying to get this record finished before…" He tried to explain but she cut him off.

"Please don't lie to me anymore. I think I've been good enough to you, for you to at least, at this point, not lie to me."

"But Renee.."

"Before you Renee me your 'brother' Lou stopped by my apartment today." She said letting him know the jig was up.

"Are you okay?"

"It's over Terrence. I brought your stuff." She said tossing his bags to the floor. "*All* of your stuff. I can't believe you would jeopardize my life by bringing drugs and guns into my home. The home I opened up to you."

She watched him as he looked at her through begging eyes. His eyes were low and red. Not only from the blunts he was smoking but from lack of sleep. He looked like he hadn't showered or shaved in days.

"Look, now isn't a good time for you to be having a moment. I just need a couple more days to get my shit together and I'll be good. I just need you to stick this out with me."

"Stick this out with you! Do you have any idea the risk you put me at? Do you! I could've lost everything."

"Look, I ran into a bad situation that I'm trying to correct. I never meant to put you in harms way. All this happened after the fact of me moving in with you." He pleaded through chapped lips as his words fell on deaf ears.

"I'm sorry Terrence." She said shaking her head.

"Look, let's go outside and talk about this." He said.

"No, there's nothing to talk about."

With annoyance in his face he grabbed her by her arm forcing her out the same way she came in.

...Constance

When Constance saw that Frog sent Derrick to inspect the shop she smiled. Deep inside she had hoped he would send him. She didn't know why but she was really starting to enjoy seeing this man.

"Are you okay?" He asked as he walked into the shop with a look of shock across his face. She could see from the sadness in his eyes he wasn't used to all this drama.

"I'm okay. Just a little shaken up with everything going on." She responded rubbing her shoulders as a chill ran up her spine. On cue he took her in his arms and held her.

"Don't worry. Everything will work itself out. Do you guys know who did this?" He asked letting her go which was the last thing she wanted him to do. Not only did he smell great but it felt great having a man hold her with so much care.

"Yeah I think it has something to do with Summer's husband." She grabbed a broom and started sweeping up the glass.

"Wait, get a bag and let's pick up the big pieces first then sweep up the rest."

He took the broom from her as she went behind the counter and got a large garbage bag. She was loving the way he was taking charge of the situation. She wondered how he felt about her as she handed him the bag. She tried to make eye contact but he was more focused on the job at hand.

"Do you think you can fix the window?"

"Nah, I don't do windows. What I can do is put up a board till she can get it fixed. I have some boards out in my truck, so once we get this all cleaned up I'll start on that."

"You can go ahead and start what you have to do and I'll clean up the glass."

"No, I want to help." He said giving her a warm smile. She smiled back and wanted to kiss him. She wasn't sure how he would react so she didn't. Instead she put on some music to keep sound in the air.

"So are you seeing anyone?" He asked catching her off guard.

"No, not right now." *Is he hitting on me?*

"So you wanna go out sometime?" He asked bending down to pick up a large piece of glass.

"Are you asking me on a date?" Constance asked being girlie.

"Why, don't date white guys?" He asked as he stood up face to face with her. The way he looked at her made her feel tingly inside and she couldn't hold it back anymore so she went for it. Much to her surprise he was a great kisser. She doesn't know how long they were kissing but they kissed until they heard a knock at the door.

"Hum excuse me are you open for business today?" A woman stood at the entrance.

"Latoya hi no, no we had an accident today so we had to close."

Constance said embarrassed.

"So should I reschedule my appointment now or later?"

"Definitely later, call and we'll do it over the phone."

"Okay, I wish somebody would've called and told me not to come."

"I'm really sorry, your next appointment will be on the house."

"Great, I'll see you then." The client said as she walked away happy.

"Maybe we should get this cleaned up so you can repair the window."

Constance felt weird now and as she bent down to start cleaning up again he grabbed her and pulled her close to him.

"Are you planning to act like that didn't just happen?"

"No."

"Okay then don't."

"So what now?" She asked looking him in his eyes as he leaned in and kissed her again.

"Now we can finish this up." He said grabbing the bag off the floor as she watched him smiling to herself. As she stood there admiring him the bus outside caught her eye. She stood there staring at an advertisement for a local news show. The thing about the advertisement that stood out was the woman's face on the side of the bus. It was the same woman she saw with Reggie that night at the club. The very same woman she saw on the tape that night having sex with him.

...Summer

As she left the precinct and headed home she was experiencing the worst headache. During questioning one of Honey's friends trying to save her own ass had disclosed helpful information pertaining to the incident. She informed the cops that in a jealous rage Honey had paid them to help her come and jump Summer. Honey had told them that Summer was jealous because her husband was leaving her and had broken her car windows. Since they had no proof of this, no one was charged with vandalizing Honey's car.

Summer couldn't help but wonder how much Honey really loved her husband. She had gone as far as risking her freedom by committing a crime in broad daylight with several witnesses on hand. Summer wondered if she, herself loved him that much. Here she was ready to end their marriage when she found out he was with another woman, while the other woman was willing to risk everything just to be with him. Summer longed for her mother to be alive as she needed someone to talk to about this other than her girlfriends.

As she entered the house through the kitchen her phone was ringing.

"Hello."

"It was her Summer, I saw her."

It sounded like Connie but she was crying so hard Summer could barely make out her voice.

"Connie?"

"Yes?"

"What happened?"

"I saw...the woman. I saw her. Oh God it was her."

"Who Connie? Who did you see?"

"It was her. It was her."

Who is her?

"Connie calm down I don't know who you're talking about."

"From the tape Summer, the woman from the tape."

"You saw her where?"

"On the bus. I saw her on the bus. Oh God I can't believe this is happening to me."

"What were you doing on the bus?"

"What? I wasn't on the bus, she was. She has a poster, she works for the news. She's an anchorwoman, I saw her poster on the side of the bus."

"Are you sure?"

"Am I sure? Of course I'm sure. It was her. I would never forget that face. It was most certainly her."

"Okay, you saw her poster on the side of a bus but what has you so upset?"

"She's better than me Summer. That's why he hasn't tried to contact me. He's with someone famous now. I can't compete with someone on television."

What?

"Constance, first off you need to calm down because you're so worked up you're not thinking straight. I wouldn't care if she was the vice president of the United States. He violated you the same way he violated her. He doesn't care what either one of you does for a living because he's still married."

Summer tried to calm herself down before she said something she would regret later. She was so sick of women who slept with married men acting as if the way they felt mattered. When it came down to it he went home to his wife. Here Constance was downing herself for a man who could care less what she did for a living. The only thing that mattered to him was getting a nut. Not her job, her feelings or her problems. None of that mattered at the end of the day.

"You're right Summer." Constance said calming down some.

"Look, I'm tired Connie. I just got home from the precinct and I really just want to lie down."

"You're home?"

"Yeah I decided to come home tonight. I really need to lay in my own bed. I have a headache and I just need to be alone tonight."

"How'd everything go at the precinct?"

"I'll tell you tomorrow. Right now I just need some rest."

As she laid in bed that night she said a silent prayer for God to bless her marriage and keep them in a safe and loving environment. Tomorrow she had a doctors appointment to find out if they were about to become parents.

...Renee

Once they made it outside the night air caught her off guard as did Terrence when he grabbed her by the neck. "Look, don't come up here acting stupid talking to me like that in front of my peoples." As he let go of her neck Renee tried to hide the fear that was racing through her body.

"Look I brought you everything that you had at my place. You forget about me and I'll forget about you." She said trying to soften the blow.

"Why can't we just talk about this?" He said abruptly changing his tone and attitude.

"There is nothing to talk about. You lied to me." She said trying to get her point across to him that it was over.

"Lied to you, I never lied to you."

"Yes, you did." She answered matter of factly.

"I never lied to you. I didn't tell you the complete truth but nothing I've told you has been a lie." He said reaching out for her. She dismissed his gesture. "Look, I'll come by once I'm done with this and we can talk about this." He said obviously not getting it.

"No! I haven't seen you in two days Terrence so you obviously have someplace to stay. I could've gone to jail, anything could've happened to me. I can't believe I was so foolish to ever get involved with someone like you in the first place." She opened her car door but before she could get in, he grabbed her by her arm.

"Don't fucking talk to me like that. Do you have any idea who the fuck I am?" He said breathing hard in her face gripping her arm tightly. She could smell the alcohol on his breath as she struggled to free herself.

"Get off of me!" She demanded as she tried to snatch her arm from the grip he had on her. She freed herself by digging her nails into his skin. She tried again to get into her car as he attempted to grab at her again. This time his hand slipped loose and she managed to reach in the car and grab her pocketbook off the seat. As he struggled to grab her she pulled out her pearl handle 22 and pointed it straight at him.

"Get the FUCK away from me!" She yelled happy that she decided to bring it with her. He backed up with his hands raised.

"Look at you. What the fuck is up with the gun?"

"Don't you ever put your fucking hands on me again."

"It's like that Renee; I can't believe you pulled a gun on me."

"Be careful who you pick up in gyms."

"Really?" He said with a faint hint of fear in his voice seeing how comfortably she held the gun.

"Yeah really."

He stood there looking at her like she was crazy. Considering it was after 3 in the morning he had no other choice but to believe she was. As he backed up putting his hands up in defeat, he walked back to the studio, to the life where he belonged.

She drove two blocks before she pulled over. She sat in her car unraveling over the night's events. Her hands shook as she tried to calm her racing heart. While she was well trained to use a firearm that was the first time she ever had to actually pull one out on someone. She couldn't help but think about Sean and even though it was the middle of the night she called him. When he answered the phone she could tell she had woken him up. Not only because it was after 3 in the morning but because it took a few minutes before he knew who he was even talking to.

"Renee?"

"Yes." She said through tears.

"What's wrong, are you okay?" He said fully awake now.

"No."

"Where are you?"

"Sean can you please come get me. I'm sorry to bother you but I don't have anybody else to call."

"Where are you?"

She gave him the address to where she was parked and waited for her knight in shining armor to come and rescue her.

...*Constance*

"Constance, Constance." She heard Derrick but she couldn't turn around. He touched her shoulder and she turned to him with tears streaming down her face.

"What happened? Was I that bad of a kisser?" He said wiping her tears.

"No, of course not." She said trying to smile. She knew she had to get herself together and fast before he thought she was psycho.

"I'm sorry. I just saw something that brought up some really bad memories."

"Are you going to be okay?"

"With you here how could I not be?"

"Are you sure?"

"Yeah lets get this mess cleaned up so we can get out of here." She said wiping the rest of her tears away.

By the time Derrick walked Constance to her door her mind was so spread out she barely thanked him for all his help.

"Are you sure you're going to be okay?" He asked, grabbing her hand. "Yeah I just need to lie down, bye."

She went into her apartment, left all the lights out and headed to her bed. She had wondered over and over again why Reggie hadn't tried to contact her. Yes she had changed her number but he knew where she lived and worked yet he never tried to contact her. What if something had happened to her or Meagan. Didn't he care to at least find out what the problem was? Now, she knew the truth. He was too busy flaunting his celebrity piece of ass around town. Not only did he cheat on her he had cheated on her with someone whose standing was higher than her own. No matter how hard she worked or how much she made she could never compete with someone who was on television. She wondered if the woman knew about the taping. Embarrassed and humiliated her self esteem was at a new low and she didn't know what else to do. So she called Summer, which wasn't of any help.

As she got off the bed and headed to the bathroom she couldn't help but want revenge on Reggie. She thought of sending the tape to the news station where the woman worked but decided not to just in case they tried to cover up the scandal. What she did decide to do was send it to a popular local tabloid show called Daily Entertainment. She knew they would love to air the news of the newswoman having an affair with the high priced married attorney. The more she thought about it the better she felt. First she would have to make a copy of the tape to edit herself out. Then she would send the copy to the show.

She figured it would be best to keep this information to herself. She could hear the smugness in Summer's voice earlier in the evening. She had spoken to Constance like she didn't mean anything to Reggie other than a piece of ass. In Constance's mind she believed she was more than that to him. It was all about image when it came to Reggie. Who could make him look good, who could help keep his name in a good light. That was one of the reasons he wouldn't divorce his wife. He was too afraid of what it would do to his image to have a divorce under his belt. Well, it was time to shake his image up a little and set the divorce papers in motion. Constance was tired of waiting for the right time, she was ready to create it.

...Summer

Lying on that table with her legs up in stirrups always made Summer feel uncomfortable no matter how many times she did it. Her doctor knowing how uncomfortable she was with it always tried to make small talk to ease the situation.

"So how's everything at work?" The gynecologist asked as she inserted the cold instrument inside of Summer.

"Well the shop is closed for renovations."

"Already? I thought you said that wouldn't take place for at least another year."

"I know, but we had a bit of an accident and my front window pane got broken so I was forced to close."

"I'm sorry to hear that." Dr. Troy said to her as she stuck the ultrasound camera between her legs. Summer closed her eyes and held her breath to take her mind off the situation.

"Okay, let's see what we see. Where's your husband today? I don't think I can ever remember him missing an appointment."

"He had some work to catch up with and he was feeling a little under the weather. Lately he has loads of work to catch up on."

"Well I guess somebody has to pay for those renovations." Dr. Troy joked.

Summer's mind began to wander. All she could think about was those business statements and all the money her husband had spent on Honey. That money was her money and he spent it on another woman. She decided to focus on the monitor to keep her mind off the elephant in the room.

"So Doc do you see anything?" She asked with a lump in her throat.

"Not yet, but you say you've been having symptoms?"

"Yeah lately I've been really nauseous."

"Get dressed. I'll be right back, okay." The doctor took off her gloves, threw them in the trash and left the room. As Summer put her clothes back on she couldn't help but think that if she was pregnant how all the money that was spent on her husbands' mistress could've gone to their child's education. All the pent up pain and frustration came flowing all over her red silk blouse. She couldn't stop the tears and she prayed at the same time for God to take away all the pain that was resting on her chest. She took a few tissues from the tissue box and cleaned her face before the doctor came back in. The look on Dr. Troy's face when she returned to the room only proved that Summer didn't do a good job at concealing it.

"Is everything okay?" Dr. Troy asked with concern as she took a seat.

"Yes, I'll be fine." She said with a forced smile.

"Are you sure? You know you can talk to me if you need to." The doctor asked again grabbing Summer's hand.

"Everything is fine. I guess my hormones are just getting the best of me." She forced an even bigger smile.

"You're sure everything is fine?" The doctor asked once more to be sure.

"Yes." Summer answered in a tone that told her to drop it.

"Okay then. Well from the results of the sonogram and blood test you're not pregnant." She knew how bad Summer wanted a baby and she wanted to make sure she took the news without a negative reaction.

"Are you sure?" Summer asked as the disappointment started to build in her throat.

"Summer, I wish I wasn't."

"But I've been…" She paused and started playing with her wedding ring.

"I know and I'm guessing it's a reaction from the hormone shots you're on, which means they're working."

"Just not good enough." The tears began to fall again.

Dr. Troy grabbed the tissue box and handed her a couple.

"Summer I told you this would take time, for some it works right away for others it takes a little bit longer. You're still young so time is on your side."

"I have to go." Summer said as she checked her face in the mirror putting on her dark colored Versace shades.

"Summer if you ever need to talk you have my number." Dr. Troy said to the back of Summer's hand as she waved goodbye on her way out.

...Renee

As Renee sat in the plush leather seats of Sean's BMW she felt so safe and secure. She wished this was a feeling she could have for the rest of her life.

"Renee, what are you doing out here this time of night?"

"I don't know Sean."

"You don't know? I just drove across town in the middle of the night and all you can come up with is I don't know?" He said looking at her with disgust.

"I know Sean, I just needed you right now." She said reaching for his hand but he moved it.

"Look Renee, I love you and I don't mind helping you but don't take my kindness for weakness. When you called me you sounded as if you had just lost a parent. Now you are going to sit here and tell me you had me drive all the way here because you *needed* me at four in the morning! Where's your man at Renee? Why didn't you call him?"

"Sean, please don't be mad with me." She massaged the back of his neck but he brushed her hand away.

"What's going on with you Renee?"

Renee knew she should've just told him the truth but it just couldn't escape her tongue. Not only would he look at her differently but that would also mean that he was right all along about Terrence. Just as he was right about her calling him to drive across town in the middle of the night just to comfort her. But she didn't care as she needed him right now. She needed to feel the security he always seemed to provide for her.

"I've been going through a lot lately Sean and it all boils down to me realizing that ending our relationship was a big mistake."

"Yeah well it's a little late for that Renee."

"No it's not Sean we still love each other."

"Yeah, well we've both moved on already so love really has nothing to do with it anymore. If love couldn't keep us together before what makes you think it will keep us together now?"

Ignoring his question she went back to what he said.

"What do you mean we both moved on? Have you met someone?" She asked thinking back to that night in his car when he was on the phone with the female caller.

"Is that important? Aren't you living with someone or rather isn't someone living with you?"

"Not anymore." She whispered.

"So is that what this is all about? Old boy ended it with you so you want to come running back to me like I'm some type of hold button."

"No Sean, you've never been my second choice." She tried to touch his face but he slapped her hand away.

"Don't touch me. Here I am risking my relationship, running out of my bed in the middle of the night for you and for what, just to realize that she was right." The last part he said more to himself than to her. His words hurt her and she knew he was right but she would never admit that to him.

"'She was right' who is she Sean and what is it that 'she's' right about?"

"This, this is what she was right about. Every time you need me I come running like we're still together. I will never be able to move on unless I let go of this first."

"I don't know who 'she' is but 'she' doesn't love you like I do."

"And she'll never get the chance if I don't let this go."

"You don't mean that."

"I love you but it's over. We both have to admit it's over."

"I'm sorry Sean but that's something I can't do." She got out of his car and got into hers. As she drove off she watched him through her rearview mirror as he put his head on the steering wheel, defeated.

...Constance

The more Constance thought about her plan the happier it made her feel as she walked to the producer's office. As she was buzzed in by his secretary her stomach did a little dance. She was more nervous than she thought she would be. When she put her hand on the knob to open the door she thought she would vomit. She had called yesterday and spoke to the producer and told him what she had. At first she was going to send it anonymously but he informed her that if he felt the tape was worth it he would pay her for it and still not reveal who submitted it. She decided it best to go in person this way she could get her check and be done with this mess once and for all. He promised her that even though he would know who she was they would not release her name to the public. She agreed and they made an appointment for this afternoon for him to view the tape.

"Hello it's nice to meet you, have a seat." Richard the producer said as he waived his hands at the chair. As he took a call Constance looked around his office which was quite plain in her opinion. She expected it to be much more glamorous, but then again she expected him to be a lot more glamorous. He was a white man in his early to mid fifties, he was bald, and his clothes were nowhere near glamorous. She forced a smile as he hung up the phone and extended his hand. She stood to shake his hand and he gave her a puzzled look.

"I wasn't asking for your hand dear, I'm asking for the tape. I'm running a business here, I don't have all day."

"Oh I'm sorry." She said reaching in her bag for the tape, a little taken back by his attitude.

"Now you said you use to date Reggie, Correct? That's how you got the tape?"

"Yes that's correct."

He took the tape from her and popped it into his player. She could tell from the sly smile on his face that he was interested in purchasing it.

"How much do you want for it?" He asked lighting a cigarette.

Damn why didn't I do research on how much these things go for.

"I was thinking $50,000 should cover it."

"$50k? You drive a hard bargain but I like what I see and I want this tape. Heather White is one of our biggest competitors. I'm willing to pay just that much. Can I write you a check?"

"As long as it won't bounce." Constance said with a smile.

When Constance got to her car and looked at the check she screamed with delight. She thought this was the easiest money that she had ever made in her life. She had never had this much money at one time. She started thinking of how she would spend the money before she even started her ignition. She decided to make a stop at Summer's house but she wouldn't tell her about the money because she knew Summer would have nothing but negative things to say about it. As she turned on 47th and Lexington making her way to the 59th street Bridge to take her back to Queens, she spotted David coming out of a bar. At first she thought she was seeing things but she wasn't. He was coming out of the bar hugged up with Honey. Not only could she not believe he was still seeing Honey but he was now hugged up with her in broad daylight. Connie wanted to approach them but she thought it best that she just mind her business. She wasn't even sure if she was going to tell Summer since they always referred to her as the bearer of bad news. As she watched them stand outside of his car hugging and kissing she wondered for the first time if David truly loved Honey. Why else would he be seen with her after all that went down. What would send him back into her arms after all of that?"

...David

As much as he loved working, sitting at home was driving him crazy. Summer was out taking care of business at the doctor and he honestly didn't feel up to going with her, so he used his injuries to get out of it. It seemed that every time they went to the doctor and she found out she wasn't pregnant they somehow ended up arguing. If they weren't arguing over giving up trying they were arguing over some new method she wanted to try to impregnate herself. He wished she would understand that it didn't matter to him if she carried the baby or not as long as they got one and got it over with.

From the look on her face when she entered the house he already knew what the results were. He wanted to get off the couch and console her but now he was in pain for real.

"Hey Pumpkin, how'd everything go?"

She ignored him which only made matters worst. She took off her shades and headed to the downstairs bathroom. He struggled off the couch and made his way to the bathroom door which was now locked.

"Summer open the door." He could hear her crying.

"No David, please just leave me alone."

"Summer we need to talk about this! Open the door!"

"I said leave me alone!"

The tone in her voice not only told him to back off but turned him off from even trying to ease her pain. It was this same attitude that drove him into the arms of another woman in the first place. As he waddled back over to the couch she came out of the bathroom and went upstairs to get in the shower. He wasn't sure if she was upset with him or at the fact that she wasn't pregnant. The distance between them was growing by the day and he wished more than anything that she didn't go to the doctor today. Things seemed to be picking up a bit between them, but after today he had come to realize that things hadn't changed much.

As he dozed off on the couch she made her way back down stairs now fully dressed in her night clothes. Her eyes were swollen from crying and she had her hair combed back, still wet from the shower. The smell of her shampoo turned him on and as she passed him he slapped her on the rear end and pulled her on top of him.

"David what are you doing?" She asked trying to get up.

"Where you trying to go? Can't you hold your husband a little?"

"I'm not in the mood David"

"Summer, you ain't never in the mood." He said immediately turned off by her attitude.

"Maybe because you're never around, maybe because you were never around or maybe because you were too busy show boating all over town with some whore." She said getting up.

"Is this how it's going to be Summer? Let me know now because I'm not going to stay here if every time you are upset you throw that shit in my face. It's either you forgive me and we move on or you don't."

"You know what David, Fuck you."

"Fuck me, Fuck you!"

Without responding she stormed off to the kitchen and he continued to watch the game. He was not about to let her and her attitude ruin his game. Twenty minutes passed and the second half of the game was about to start when he heard a dish break in the kitchen. As he struggled off the couch to make sure everything was okay Summer stormed out of the kitchen throwing dishes at him screaming.

"Why the fuck can't you clean up after yourself?" She threw a dirty plate at him that he ducked from as it crashed against the wall.

"What the fuck is wrong with you!" He screamed at her.

"You have been in here all fucking day and you expect me to come home and clean up after you! That's why we aren't able to have kids, you're a big damn kid yourself!" She threw the glass she had in her other hand at him. The glass bounced off his arm and crashed on the floor.

"You have lost your fucking mind." He struggled to put his slippers on and headed to his car where he always kept an extra set of clothes and shoes.

      As he drove down the highway doing 80 his mind was all over the place. He couldn't understand why no matter how hard he tried his wife couldn't be happy. These were some of the reasons he didn't stop seeing Honey and this were part of the very reason he was calling her now.

"Hello."

She answered sounding sexy as ever, just hearing her voice made his dick hard. After all that went down he didn't want to say the wrong thing.

"What are you wearing sexy?"

"Anything you want."

He could hear her smile through the phone.

"I guess that means nothing at all."

"If that's what you want."

"I want to see you."
"You've got to be kidding me."

"Meet me at our spot in ½ hour."

"What if I don't?"

"Then I'll expect you needed time to freshen up and I'll see you in 45 minutes." He hung up smiling knowing fully well she would meet him there or else she wouldn't have answered her phone. His number was programmed in her phone and he knew she checked her caller ID prior to answering so he was sure she would meet him.

...Summer

She was so sure this time that she was pregnant. In her heart she felt that after all that had went down that God would finally bless her with a child. To learn that she wasn't pregnant was a reality check that her marriage may not survive. In her mind they needed that baby to start over, to get them over the null in their marriage. They needed something to bring them together and now in her eyes they had nothing.

As she parked her car in the driveway she sat for 10 minutes contemplating the future of her marriage. She knew David would give her a song and dance about giving up and trying to adopt. That was always his answer to them not getting pregnant. He didn't grasp that she wanted to know what it felt like to bond with the baby prior to it being born. She longed to feel a baby grow inside of her again and adoption would not give her that option. Until her doctor told her she needed to give up, she was willing to continue to try.

When she entered the house and saw how calm and relaxed he was it only made matters worst. She heard him saying something but she just ignored him and went to the bathroom to run some water on her face. Looking at herself in the mirror she began to feel both helpless and worthless. David started knocking on the door trying to see what was wrong but he already knew. Right now all she wanted to do was be left alone. She wasn't in the mood to be comforted. She went upstairs to take a shower trying her best to get on with her life. By the time she got of out the shower she began to feel better. She slipped on her bathrobe and headed to the kitchen to start dinner.

When she got downstairs she was in no mood to fool around with David. As she entered the kitchen and saw the mess that he left, an anger came over her that she couldn't control anymore. When he got up and left she felt happy and relieved and that's when she knew their marriage was over. Her doctor told her stress would interfere with nature and he was bringing a lot of that into their marriage lately.

She got the broom and dustpan and cleaned up the mess she made. Her phone rang but she refused to answer it. She wasn't in the mood to speak to anybody right now. She poured herself a drink put on some music and for the first time in a long time had a nice, peaceful night, alone.

...Renee

As Renee sat in her car outside of Sean's job she contemplated what she was going to say. For the past three days she had tried to reach him by phone but he wouldn't answer or return any of her calls. Thus, she decided to take off work today and pay him a visit at the office. Now that she was here she was nervous and couldn't come up with what to say once inside. She tried to call Summer for advice but she had not answered or returned her calls either. She had hoped that Summer could come with her for moral support but now she was on her own.

She stepped out the car wearing a brand new silk pastel pink Ralph Lauren signature summer dress that crossed her chest and tied at the waist with a matching belt that revealed her cleavage. She checked her hair and makeup to make sure they were in place and threw on her Burberry shades. As she entered the office all eyes were on her as the attention boosted her fragile ego and gave her the confidence she needed to confront Sean. She had grown tired of all the back and forth. She wanted him and was ready to prove it. At the same time she needed to make him realize that he only wanted her as well.

All the confidence in the world didn't prepare her for the butterflies that were in her stomach as she knocked on the door. It was the middle of the day and Stacey, his secretary was out to lunch just as she expected her to be. When his office door opened she had the biggest smile plastered on her face mirrored by the biggest look of shock on his.

"Renee what are you doing here?"

"I came to talk to you, aren't you going to invite me in?

"Talk about what?"

"Well, if you invite me in we can talk about it."

"Lets make this quick, I have somewhere to be."

As she entered his office she noticed that the picture he used to have prominently on his desk of the two of them was no longer there.

"Did you get rid of all my pictures at the house too?" she asked pointing to the empty space on his desk.

"Why are you here?"

"Why haven't you returned any of my calls?"

"Why are you here?"

"Do you hate me Sean? Is that it?"
"Renee, I'm going to ask you one more time because I have somewhere to be. Why are you here?"

"I came to see you Sean. I needed to see you."

"See me for what?"

She didn't know what to say. She had come all this way and was now at a loss for words. She had no idea what she could say to fix all that had occurred. She didn't know how to express to him how much she loved him or how much she was committed to changing to prove it to him.

"Sean, I don't know what to say."

"That's because there is nothing left to say. It's over and we both need to realize that. You coming here is not going to make things any better for either of us."

"But I don't want it to be over, can't you see that? I still love you. You are the only man that I have ever really loved." She wasn't expecting to be that candid but once she started she couldn't stop herself.

"Most of my life I've been trying to avoid loving somebody as much as I love you because of what my father did to my mother. The way my mother loved him I could never understand why he would hurt her the way he did.

After seeing my mother go through that pain I vowed to never love a man to the point that he could tear me down by rejecting that love. Sean, I love you that much and it scared me. It scared me to the point that I couldn't handle it. I thought being with other men would make it right, but in the end I ended up doing to you what my father did to my mother, so I'm sorry."

Bringing up her past was something Renee rarely did.

"Renee, you don't have to do this." Sean said fully aware of this fact.

"Yes I do. I need you to know that what I did was not to hurt you but to keep myself from getting hurt. The thing I failed to realize is that you aren't my father and I'm not my mother. The thing I couldn't see is that you love me and that I love you. I love you Sean and I can't just walk away from this relationship like I don't." She said as the words flowed freely from her soul.

Just as he was about to respond a knock came at the door and a woman peeked her head in. Since Renee was standing behind the door all she saw was the back of the woman's head and the woman didn't see her at all… at first.

"Hey, you ready for lunch?" She asked with a smile until she saw the look on his face. "Is everything okay?" She asked concerned. Upon entering the office she saw Renee standing there.

"Oh, I didn't know you had company." The woman said with a slight attitude. Renee could tell from the uncomfortable look on Sean's face that this was the woman occupying his time. Tracy was the total opposite of Renee. She was about 5'2, light skin and frail thin. She was pretty if you liked that type of woman but Renee knew she was more of Sean's type.

"Um yeah, Tracy this is Renee, Renee, Tracy."

"His girlfriend." Tracy said inching closer to him.

Renee, not feeling the least bit intimidated smiled and politely said.

"Funny that you claim to be his girlfriend, but I'm wearing his ring." And glowingly flashed her diamond.

"I guess that's because you were too tacky to give it back." Tracy said becoming upset.

"If that helps you sleep better at night baby girl." She walked over to Sean carefully avoiding any physical contact with Tracy and kissed him good bye. "I'll speak to you later."

As she left the office she could hear Tracy say. "I know that bitch didn't just kiss you on the mouth in front of me." She smiled to herself because she knew, he knew and even Tracy knew that he enjoyed every second of the kiss. She only hoped that she laid enough ground for him to forgive her and allow them to start anew.

Part Three:

Make it to

Heaven

...Constance

It was Sunday night and Derrick was over for dinner. Constance had invited him over to make up for the way she behaved when he dropped her off. She hadn't really seen much of him or anybody for that matter since leaving the producer's office. She was experiencing so many feelings about the situation. At first she was excited about the revenge, and then happy about the money, then regretful for the act of vengeance and ultimately, confused. Now she was just ready to get it over with. She had watched the show all month but they still had yet to air the tape. While one part of her wished they would never air it, another part of her yearned for the moment they did.

Derrick sat on the couch watching the basketball game snacking on some chips and dip she set out for him. Her daughter was at her mother's house for the weekend and Constance didn't plan to get her until the following night. She decided to make fried chicken since that was one of the only things she could cook without ruining it. She made sure to pick up a large order of rice at the Chinese restaurant earlier in the day. She put it in a pot to make it look as if she had prepared it herself. Constance was a lot of things but a cook she was not. As she watched him enjoy the game a warm feeling in her heart turned into a broad smile. This was a feeling she hadn't felt in some time and it felt good.

"Derrick would you like a beer?"

"Yeah."

She got him a beer from the fridge and as she handed it to him she held onto it just a little longer so she could stare into his eyes.

"Thank you." He said with a smile. She smiled back and went to finish preparing the chicken. The ringing of the phone interrupted her.

"Hello." She answered a little too excited. She smiled as she caught herself.

"Hey girl it's Renee."

Renee? What the hell is she calling me this time of night for? I haven't spoken to her in a couple of weeks.

"Is everything okay Renee?"

"Yeah everything's fine."

"So what's up?"

"I wanted to talk to you about something but not over the phone. Do you think I can stop by?"

"When?"

"Tonight."

"No."

"Okay how about we meet for lunch tomorrow? Is the baby home this weekend I would love to take her shopping."

"No, she's at my mother's house. Where'd you want to meet and what is this about?"

"Let's meet in the city somewhere and I'll tell you tomorrow when I see you. I'll call you in the morning and let you know where we can meet. I have to stop by the office so maybe I'll just pick you up. okay?"

"Okay."

"Good, then I'll see you tomorrow." She hung up without saying goodbye.

I wonder what this is about.

As she sat and watched Derrick eat she couldn't help but feel warm and excited inside. It had been weeks since she had sex and was secretly hoping that her dry spell would end tonight.

"How's the food?"

"It's good and might I add you look great in that dress."

She was wearing a short black mini dress that showed off her legs. Since she was short she wore a pair of 4" heals that gave her the extra height and the sexiness needed to pull of an outfit like this. Her hair was pulled up and bobby pinned.

"I feel guilty having you stay in looking as good as you do." He said biting his bottom lip.

"Don't feel guilty. I would much rather be in here with you than to have to share you with anybody out there." She said as she mattered her lipstick.

"Don't worry. If we were out my eyes would only be for you."

"Are you trying to make me blush?"

Derrick got up, walked over and gently kissed her. As she felt his tongue dance around in her mouth her whole body felt on fire. She didn't know if it was the champagne or the way he smelled but she had a thumping in between her legs that needed to be soothed. As he started to back away she pulled him back and guided his hand up her dress to expose that she wore a garter and no panties. As he played around inside of her she could feel their breathing intensify. As he kissed her she loosened his pants and found what she was looking for. She was happy to find that the myth was not true in his case. As she caressed his manhood he moaned in ecstasy and tilted his head back. When he brought his head forward his mouth found her breast and he sucked and caressed her nipples as she nibbled on his neck and ear.

"I want you now." She moaned in his ear. He took her by surprise when he stood up, lifted her, and found his way to her bed. He laid her on the bed and slowly undressed her, first taking off her shoes. As he massaged and sucked on her feet Constance felt as if she was in heaven. No man had ever sucked on her toes before and she was so glad she kept her manicure and pedicure game up to par. After he finished with her feet he worked his tongue up her leg and nibbled on her inner thigh, causing her to squirm and laugh out loud. As he found his way further up she held her breath in anticipation until the moment his mouth found what it was looking for. She exhaled, moaned out and clutched the back of his head. *If awards were given out for this he would get first prize.* She thought as she anticipated returning the favor. Without missing a beat she positioned herself on top of him so she could do just that. For the next two hours they showed each other just how much they needed one another.

...Summer

It had been two weeks since Summer left the house and even longer since she answered the phone or even checked her messages. She and David were like two ships passing in the night. With the shop closed she had nothing to do most of the time. Thus, she just sulked around the house in her pajamas. As she lay in bed watching TV and eating ice cream, David had walked in earlier than he had been lately. Their marriage had virtually fallen apart.

"What are you still doing up?" He asked taking off his shoes.

"I'm usually up at this hour, but how would you know when you're hardly home at this hour."

"Not tonight Summer. Please, can we go one night without fighting?"

"Whatever."

"So what did you do today?"

"Exactly what I'm doing now."

"Baby, you haven't been out in days. Have you even spoken to Constance?"

"No."

"Why do you insist on being depressed? When are you going to open the shop back up?"

"What the fuck do you care David?"

"You know Summer, maybe if you changed your attitude we could get along better. I come home early trying to bond with you and look at the attitude I get. How do you expect us to get pregnant if we can't even get along long enough to have sex?"

"David please."

"Please what Summer? I'm trying to make this work the best I can but I can't do it alone."

"You cheated alone."

"Oh please would you get off of that. How long are you going to hold that shit against me? What the fuck do you want me to do, cut off my right arm?"

"Maybe your dick." She said still staring at the screen.

"I'll be downstairs. I can't deal with this shit. And you wonder why I don't like coming home anymore."

As he left the room Summer couldn't help but feel a little guilty. Even when he was trying, she was so out of it that she couldn't will herself to be nice anymore. As she got out of bed and dragged herself in front of the mirror, the image she saw staring back frightened her. She was turning into an old bat before her time. The heavy bags under her eyes and the wild hair atop her head only proved it. She swallowed her wounded pride and made her way downstairs to find David on the couch already asleep. She took advantage of this time and went upstairs to shower and put on a sexy nighty. She washed her hair using the shampoo that drove him crazy.

As she made her way back downstairs she made sure to be quiet so she wouldn't wake him. He already had his clothes off and was laying in his boxer shorts. She got on her knees next to the couch and let his manhood find its way into her mouth. She played around with him until he was erect and she took it from there. As he moaned half asleep he was shocked to wake up and find his wife was the one bringing him this pleasure. The shock alone almost caused him to erupt in her mouth but he controlled himself and enjoyed the pleasure that she was bringing him. As he grabbed her wet hair she knew she had accomplished what she set out to do. She decided to add a little spice and shock to what had become a broken spirit and marriage. As he begged her to stop she sucked harder till he was finally able to pull her loose. He turned her around and entered where she had never let him enter before. The pain was both excruciating and pleasurable at the same time. She tried to fight but the more she fought the deeper he went. Once he felt she had been punished enough for all the pain and suffering she caused over the past few weeks he entered her womanhood. They didn't make love but "fucked" for the first time in their relationship After they finished she laid staring at the ceiling smiling, as she had loved every minute of it.

...Renee

Since Renee visited Sean at his office she knew she had a lot of work to do. Even with all the confidence she had, Tracy was now with Sean and she wasn't a bad piece of arm candy at that. A little on the skinny side but she could give Renee a run for her money. She had to devise a plan to get him back and she planned on using Constance to help her. Given their close relationship she figured that Constance would have some information on Tracy and how serious Sean was about her.

She was leaving her office on her way to pick up Constance so they could go grab a bite to eat. She was wearing a pair of fitted 7 jeans with a white Polo Tee and white stiletto tie up sandals. Her hair was in a ponytail and in desperate need of being done. She didn't know what was going on with Summer but if she didn't get it together soon Renee was going to have to find a new stylist. The window in the shop was fixed last week, so she wondered why Summer still hadn't opened back up for business. Had she given up hope for the shop because she couldn't get pregnant? Renee was happy she didn't have that damn mama bug flowing through her blood. She could care less if she had a child or not. Her focus right now was on getting her man back and making things right between them. Then maybe she could focus on things like kids, but until then that was not a priority. As she pulled up in front of the house Constance was already outside waiting. Renee couldn't help but admire the pink DKNY jogging suit Constance had on. She even had on a pair of matching DKNY shades and tennis shoes. The glow coming from her when she got in the car was not from all the pink she had on. She had a smile plastered on her face that could light up the tree at Rockefeller center.

"Well hello."

"Hi."

"What are you so happy about?"

"Nothing."

"Yeah right nothing. Did I just miss Reggie?"

The look that Constance gave her let her know that her happiness had nothing to do with Reggie.

"Okay, I'll get it out of you later." She said as she drove off.

"So where are we going?"

"I was thinking we could go to City Island since it's such a beautiful day. Are you in the mood for seafood?"

"Sure, it doesn't matter to me."

As they found a place to eat Renee still wasn't sure if Constance would help her but after about 15 minutes of filler talk, she figured what the hell. It wasn't like she had many options in the matter.

"So how has everything been going?" She decided to start off light.

"Nothing much Stop beating around the bush and spit it."

"What?" Renee tried to play dumb but Constance just stared at her.

"Okay, it's about Sean."

"Of course it is, what about him?"

"I don't know if you know, but he's seeing somebody."

"Yes, I think her name is Tracy."

Hearing Tracy's name sent fury through Renee's blood.

"Yeah that's her name. You know her?"

"No I don't know her, but I've met her."

"Look I'm not going to beat around the bush. I want Sean back, I want her tired ass out the picture and I need your help."

"My help? What can I do to help?"

"First off, what do you know about this chick?"

"Not much. He met her a month or two ago through a friend. I think she's about 22 or 23."

"She's that young?"

"Yeah, I think she works on 5th Avenue in one of those clothing stores."

"Doing what?"

"Sales girl I think. When we met she offered me a discount but I wasn't paying her much attention."

"Do you think he's serious about her?" Renee's stomach was in knots awaiting an answer.

"I don't know Renee. I mean he doesn't introduce me to a lot of girls but then again he's been with you for awhile so I really can't say."

"Well then guess Connie. This means a lot to me."

"I can't say Renee. I guess he's dating her to get over you."

"So you think I still have a chance?"

"At what?"

"At getting him back."

"I thought you moved on. What happened with your man?"

"Never mind that, it's over, that's all that matters. I love Sean and I'm willing to do whatever it takes to be with him."

"So what do you want me to do?"

"Help me get him back."

"How? I can't control who he wants to be with."

"Connie this means a lot to me. I love Sean. I know I fucked up but I'm willing to right that wrong if he gives me the chance."

"So again, what do you think I can do?"

"First, I need you to find out how serious he is about this chick. Then I need you to remind him of how much we love each other. I need you to plant that seed that we were made for each other. Make him realize that we need to be together and that being with her is just an attempt to get over me."

"You really do love him."

"More than I ever knew. I fucked up Connie, big time. God made me realize it too. If it's true that you only get one true love in life I know he's it. I almost lost him because I let my own insecurities get in the way. I can't lose him Connie."

"I hate to say this, but what if you already have."

"Not to be full of myself but I haven't. Sean loves me just as much as I love him. The only difference is he was in touch with his feelings long before I was."

"Fine then, I'll help you in whatever way I can."

Renee was shocked that Constance was so easily persuaded. She was sure she would have to beg her to help. Something was definitely going on in Constance's life and she liked it, whatever it was. If things worked out or didn't Renee acknowledged that she would forever be indebted to Constance for putting their differences aside and looking out for her.

...Constance

Before today Constance would never have considered helping Renee. But she knew that if Renee felt for Frog the way she felt for Derrick she didn't want to interfere but rather help bring it together. After their love making episode last night he stayed over. When they woke up he took her to IHOP for breakfast. She loved everything about him, the way he smelled, smiled, his walk, his eyes and of course the way he made her feel. It was like nothing she ever felt before. For the first time in her life she felt like she was in love.

"So what has you on cloud nine today?" Renee asked stuffing her face with lobster.

"I think I might be in love." Constance said with a giggle.

"What? With who?"

"Derrick."

"Who?"

"Derrick, the guy from Ohio that works with for Frog."

"The white dude."

"Yes the white dude. Do you have to refer to him like that?"

"Well, sorry. What happened with Reggie?"

"Too much to talk about, but it's over between us."

"Did it have anything to do with that woman at the club that night?"

"Something but not everything I don't want to talk about Reggie. It's over so he's not worth my breath."

"Okay, so what made you want to get with Derrick?"

"Look Renee, lets get this straight right now because I hear the sarcasm in your voice. I know how you feel about interracial dating. Everybody is not your parents. I understand your feelings but the same way you want me to respect your love for Frog please respect my feelings for Derrick. It shouldn't matter what color his skin is. All that matters is he makes me happy. Happier than any man I've been with in a long time."

"You're right and I apologize. From the time I pulled up you've had this look on your face that I've never personally seen before. So if he's the one that brings you there then I'm happy for you."

"Thank you." Constance said as she answered her ringing phone.

"Hello."

"Hey girl what's up?"

"You tell me stranger where the fuck have you been?"

"I've been around."

"Well I've been calling you like crazy. I even stopped by the house but nobody answered the door. I almost called the cops."

"I just needed some time to get my thoughts together. Where are you?"

"In City Island with Renee."

"Really, tell her I said hello. I was about to call her but I'll just call her later. I wanted to call and let you know I'm going to open the shop up tomorrow."

"Renee, its Summer, she said to tell you hi and that she's opening the shop tomorrow."

"Good, because I was about to find another stylist tell her I said she could pick up a phone and return some of my calls, damn."

"She heard you. She's laughing. She said come by the shop tomorrow and she'll make it up to you."

"All right I'll see you tomorrow. It's nice to hear from you again."

"I love yall. See you tomorrow."

"What the fuck has been up with her?" Renee asked in disgust.

"I think she found out she wasn't pregnant again."

"She needs to let that shit go already. Not having a baby is not the end of the world."

"But not getting Frog is?"

"Point taken."

"We all have our own wants and needs and this is something she wants and needs. Thank you God for finally giving me what I needed." She said with a smile big enough to light the sky.

...Summer

Since Summer opened the shop back up she was feeling better than she felt in months. She had no idea how much she enjoyed working until she stopped. She missed her friends and clients and it was so good to see Constance with this aura of positively. For as long as she knew Constance she never remembered her being so happy. She was even spending more time with her daughter which made Summer very happy. She had to admit Derrick did seem like a Godsend in Constance's life. Renee had even seemed to change over the past summer. She wasn't sure what happened with Terrence but she was happy it was over. There was something about him that rubbed her the wrong way. She knew that Renee's heart was still with Frog, she just hoped that this new girl Frog was seeing hadn't already filled the void left by Renee. As far as her marriage went they were still trying their best to make it work. David had even come home before 12 everyday this past week which in his case was a big improvement.

"Summer, did you ever find out who busted your window out?" Daisy, a customer getting her hair braided asked.

"A jealous hoe." Constance answered.

"Well, I hope you're going to press charges."

"I'm still thinking about it." Summer said.

"Thinking about it?" Constance asked with an attitude.

"Yes Constance, thinking about it. We aren't all innocent in this either."

Summer said as she was curling her clients' hair.

"Whatever. If it was me I would press charges."

"Well David and I have been talking about it and we are just ready to move on with our life."

"Like I said, whatever." Constance said rolling her eyes.

"Shoot, a bitch better not ever cross you Connie." Her client said laughing.

"You damn right about that." She said giggling with her.

"Constance please, you crossed enough people in your life time to let some shit slide." Summer said as she sprayed hair sheen.

It was 6:00 when the bell chimed indicating someone was entering the shop. The last three customers looked up to see Renee enter wearing a baby blue silk pant suit. Her hair was still fresh from the weave Summer put in earlier in the week. Today she wore it up which showed off the diamond chain and matching earrings she wore. She was carrying a Marc Jacobs clutch bag. Summer smiled when she saw Renee walk in. Summer knew that with all the glitz and glamour she tried to project that there was pain hiding behind those shades. Until she was named Mrs. Sean Billings she would never be completely happy. Constance had finally talked to Frog for Renee and he agreed to meet her for dinner tonight. As bold and beautiful as Renee tried to act Summer knew below the surface she was scared to death to lose him.

"Evening ladies." She said with a smile plastered on her face.

"Hey girl." Constance said kissing her on the cheek. Summer was happy to *finally* see the two of them getting along.

"You look cute." Summer said giving her a hug.

"Do you think I need to redo my makeup?"

"Didn't I just say you look cute."

"I know. I just need everything to be perfect."

"I see you brought out the big dogs." Constance said admiring her diamond set.

"Yeah he bought this for me for my birthday last year."

"Don't worry everything is going to be fine." Summer said with a smile.

"I hope so. You got any champagne in the fridge?"

"I think so, go check."

"So Connie what'd he say about us meeting?" She asked as she checked the fridge.

"Come on Renee, didn't we already go over this."

"Well tell me again damn it." She said pouring herself a drink.

"He said he had no problem meeting you."

"Did he seem like he looked forward to seeing me?"

"I don't know."

"You are no help."

"You'll find out what's up tonight so just chill out."

"Isn't that his car outside?" Summer asked smiling.

"Ah shit he's early." Renee said finishing her drink running to the bathroom to check her makeup.

When Summer saw Frog enter the shop she could see why Renee was such a nervous wreck. Frog was a fine man standing at 6'4". His hazel brown eyes were sparkling next to his caramel complexion. His teeth were a beautiful shade of white as he flashed his smile at the ladies in the shop, talking on his cell phone. Once he finished his call he made his rounds saying hello to everyone.

"I know I'm early but I got out of my meeting early so I decided to head straight here." He said giving Summer a hug.

"Is Derrick still at work?" Constance said finishing her customer's hair.

"Yes Constance he is." He said giving her a big smile. "You got my man's head all open. You take it easy on the country boy."

"Shut up Frog." Constance said laughing. As they sat around laughing Renee came out of the bathroom.

...Renee

Walking out of the bathroom and seeing him in his beige Sean John Denim shorts and cotton top setting off his white on white air force ones she knew she had to do everything in her power tonight to make this man hers, again. She flashed him her best smile as she walked over and greeted him with a kiss. She couldn't help but notice he was wearing the cologne she brought him.

"You look nice." He said smiling at her.

"Thank you, you don't look bad yourself."

"You two look great together." Summer's client said getting her hair blown out.

"Thank you." Renee said smiling.

"Are you ready?" He asked touching the side of her face sending chills through her.

"Yeah." She said with a smile.

"Have fun you two and do everything I wouldn't." Summer joked as they exited the shop.

They ended up going to a trendy restaurant on the lower east side. Renee was happy he chose this place because it was quiet and not too crowded. It was more romantic than friendly and she hoped this was a good sign. On one hand he could be trying to be romantic while on the other he could have chosen this place just in case she decided to make a scene when he let her down. The ride in the car didn't reveal much of how he was feeling because he spent the majority of the time on the phone conducting business. He was starting a new building in the coming weeks and he had to make sure he had all the necessary permits and materials for the job. She was relieved when he left the phone in the car. At least that wouldn't be a distraction.

Once the hostess sat them and they put in their orders Renee felt an uncomfortable silence.

"Why are you so quiet?" He asked breaking the silence.

"Nervous."

"The diva's nervous? I'm shocked."

"Don't make fun Sean."

"I'm serious."

"Well, you make me nervous."

"All of a sudden you're nervous around me."

"I guess I'm more nervous about what needs to be discussed than I am of being around you."

"Well what is it you want to discuss?" He asked grabbing her hand.

"Why did you agree to meet me tonight?" She said changing the subject.

"Well Connie and I were talking about how we used to all hang out and how so much has changed over this past summer. She was telling me that yall had lunch which was a shock since you two had become really distant. She was explaining to me how much change and growth she saw in you and she suggested that we try to mend our friendship if nothing else."

Hearing him say friendship caused her to pull her hand from his grip.

"I didn't know we had a friendship."

"Renee we were in love or at least I thought we were. How can there be love with no friendship?"

"You know what I meant."

"No, why don't you try explaining." He said as he poured them a glass of champagne from the bottle the waitress set beside the table on the ice bucket stand.

"Do you still love me?"

"I will always love you Renee."

"Don't patronize me Sean, you know what I mean."

"Then say what you mean Renee."

"Are you still seeing Tracy?"

"After that afternoon in my office things kind of slowed down. Not to mention all the time I've been spending at work. I think it's too much for her to handle. She has this crazy notion that I'm lying about work to be with you."

Renee couldn't help but to blush at that statement.

"I never took that to be your type."

"What type?"

"Insecure."

"To be honest, it's not. I didn't take her to be the insecure type either until after that day, but I guess you have that effect on people. Your confidence can be a little intimidating."

"Is that a bad thing?"

"Depends on who you're asking."

"I'm asking you."

"No not me. I actually find it sexy. It's one of your better qualities."

"And my worst would be."

"Your fear to be loved."

Renee, at a lost for words sipped on her drink until the food arrived. For the rest of the night they made small talk about friends, family and work. The need to discuss them as a couple never came up again and Renee thought maybe it was best this way. If she could only have Sean in her life as friend then that is what she was willing to accept.

...Summer

It was Friday night and Summer was finally finished with work. As she and Constance cleaned and counted the money made from the day she was beginning to come full circle. She had come to accept the fact that if she if she couldn't have a baby then she would learn to appreciate everything else that she did have in her life.

"Are you going to get Meagan after this?"

"Nah, Derrick is going to pick her up from my mother's house. They're going to swing by here and pick me up."

"Wow, he's really a good dude isn't he?"

"Summer, I feel so blessed to have him in my life. My whole family loves him, including Meagan. I never would've thought I could be this happy with a man, yet I am. I swear it scares me sometimes. It's like nothing this good comes without a price."

"Maybe you already paid the price and this is your reward."

"One can only hope."

"Well he seems like a good man to me."

"We have been inseparable since we got together. He's been over to my place every night and I'm loving it." She said with glee.

"I'm happy for you, I really am."

"So how's everything with you and David going?"

"Surprisingly it's going okay. Knock on wood." As she went to knock on the desk a glimpse on the muted television caught her eye.

"Oh my goodness where's the remote, where's the remote?"

"What happened?" Constance said as she turned to look at the television to see Reggie's face plastered across the screen.

"Isn't that Reggie?" Summer asked turning up the volume. She looked just in time to see the color leave Constance's face as she stood there with her mouth held open. The reporter was telling a tale of the high priced attorney who was gallivanting all over town with a local anchorwoman while his unsuspecting wife played Polly homemaker. They even had pictures of his wife shopping and running errands while they showed him dipping in and out of limos and hotels with his mistress. "Coming up next is exclusive footage more shocking than the rest. If you have young children at home, we'd advise you to send them to the next room." The newscaster said teasing the television audience. As they were going into commercial they showed a brief clip of a blurred out couple that appeared to show them in a compromising position. They were going to show the tape.

"Oh my goodness Constance isn't that the place we were at?" Summer asked a stunned Constance. Constance just stood there staring at the television motionless.

"Are you alright?" Summer asked. This time she noticed her friend was shaking. "Connie calm down, it's okay. Do you think that's a copy of the same tape you have?" Connie just shook her head yes. "Oh goodness lets just pray you aren't on it."

...Constance

Even though Constance knew she was the one who submitted the tape and that it would one day in fact be aired she was just as shocked as Summer was watching it. She had been so caught up in her own world that she stopped checking for promos as to when the show would be aired. She now knew what took them so long to air the tape. They were doing background research on Reggie and his lover. Not only did they show them together eating dinner and going in and out of hotels together. They even tried to interview them on separate occasions but neither had a comment and denied the rumors. They did a cut and edit of them having sex so every time one would deny the rumor they would flash a scene. When they talked about Reggie's life they showed photos of him and his family coming from church together then they would flash back to the sex tape. Seeing Patty still turned Constance's stomach except she felt sorry for her now. If she was in Patty's shoes she would be devastated. She couldn't even imagine something like that happening to her and Derrick.

"I wonder where they got that footage from." Summer said interrupting her thought. Constance just shrugged her shoulders and didn't dare look at her because she just might see the guilt in her eyes.

"Maybe you should call him and make sure he's doing okay."

"I don't think so. Why would I call him?"

"I don't know because he's going through a hard time right now."

"Well trust me I'm the last person he wants to hear from right now."

"Why would you say that? According to you, you guys were in love."

"Well that was then and this is now. I haven't spoken to Reggie since that night and I don't think it's wise to speak to him now."

"I don't get it. I thought you took the master tape. How could they have gotten a copy of that?"

"Maybe mine was the copy." Constance said wishing Summer would stop trying to play detective. "But how? He left before you did and you were the last person on the tape. When would he have had time to make a copy?"

"Well maybe he copied the part with him and her before I came, who knows, who cares? They've been outted and I just hope my name doesn't become involved in all this mess." She meant that part.

"Why would it? You already took the tape." Summer said looking at her with suspicious eyes. Constance was more than happy when Derrick and Meagan came into the shop.

"Hi mommy, Derrick bought me a movie." Meagan said giving her a kiss.

"I told you, you don't have to keep buying her things."

"And I told you, you can't tell me what to do with my money." He said kissing her on the cheek. "Meagan I don't get a hug and kiss?" Summer asked.

"Of course you do. I like to save the best for last." Meagan said giving her what she asked for. "You ready to go?" Derrick asked. "Yep, Summer I'll see you tomorrow." Constance said as she gathered her things and headed home with her family.

...Renee

As Renee worked out she kept one eye open hoping that she wouldn't run into Terrence. She hadn't seen or heard from him since that night at the studio and she hoped it stayed that way. She figured he was probably afraid she would call Lou or contact the police that he likely forgot about her.

On the other hand her dinner last night with Sean was really all she could think about. That is what brought her to the gym this morning to work out. She was really trying to keep her mind occupied but it wasn't working. When he dropped her off last night he walked her to her building and gave her a really big hug, but no kiss.

When Renee reached her building from the gym she was exhausted and ready to hit the sack. She was shocked when her doorman handed her a box of roses. She couldn't wait to get upstairs and read the card. She was sure they were from Sean and sure enough they were. As she brought one of the roses up to her nose and inhaled it she smiled to herself. She couldn't help but think of how a few months ago this gesture had turned her off. She felt like a school girl with a crush as she read the card enclosed.

Last night was great.

Can't wait to see you again.

She couldn't believe he wanted to see her again. She jumped up and down and did a dance on her way to her room to find something to wear for the next time they met.

Later that evening as she cleaned her house singing along to her Anita Baker Rapture CD the ringing of her doorbell caught her off guard. She checked the peep hole hoping it wasn't Terrence or worst his friend Lou looking for him. She jumped back when she saw it was Sean. She didn't want him to see her looking like this. She had on a pair of sweat pants, a tee shirt and her hair was in a pony tail. He rung the bell again and she had no choice but to open the door.

"I brought Chinese." He said holding up a bag.

"I wasn't expecting to see you today." She said locking the door behind him.

"Did I interrupt something?" He asked looking around and she knew then that he was making a surprise visit to see if she was seeing someone else.

"Cleaning as you can tell." She said referring to her clothes.

"I think you look beautiful."

"Ha, ha let me go slip something on."

He grabbed her arm as she tried to head towards the back.

"Please don't."

"But Sean look at me."

"I am."

"Fine then." She said heading to the kitchen to get some plates to eat off of.

When she returned from the kitchen he had all the lights out. He was drawing her blinds to make it as dark inside the apartment as possible.

"What are you doing?" She asked knowing fully well what he was doing.

"Just sit down." He said not even looking at her as he worked. She did as she was told. She watched him as he headed to her linen closet and pulled out a blanket and set it on the floor. He went into her bathroom and got four candles to set the mood as she sat watching him smiling. "You ready to eat?"

She shook her head smiling she was truly at a loss of words. They sat down and ate Chinese under candle light.

...Summer

As Summer finished cleaning the shop she couldn't shake the thought that Constance had something to do with that tape being leaked to the media. She was about to turn the lights out when someone knocked on the door startling her. She was going to yell out that she was closed when she noticed it was the investigator that she hired to spy on her husband. As she headed to the door she kicked herself in the ass. Over the past few weeks he had left her several messages asking her to contact him. He wanted to know if she still needed his services and if she didn't she should call him and let him know so he could close her case and give her the final bill. He must've gotten impatient and decided to come to her; as she opened the door she smiled and apologized.

"I'm so sorry I haven't returned your calls. I've been going through some things and I'm actually just getting back on my feet." She said showing him a seat.

"It's perfectly fine. I just wanted to see where we stand as far as the case goes because until you tell me to close the case I'm still working and billing you."

"Well I don't think there is much work left to do so I guess we can close the case."

"I thought you would say that so I brought everything for you. I just need you to sign a few release papers and our business will be done."

"I'm sorry you had to come all the way down here."

"Oh it's no problem. I was in the area on an assignment so I figured I would kill two birds with one stone."

"Not on my case I hope."

"No not tonight." He went in his briefcase and handed her a few papers to sign. Once that was done he handed her a large manila envelope.

"Would you like for me to go over everything with you or can you take it from here?"

"I must admit I'm a little confused as to what all of this is? My husband stopped seeing Honey over a month ago."

"And you say this because?"

"I say it because of a lot of reasons. I've been going through hell these past couple of months and my life is finally coming together."

"I understand."

"No you don't." She responded quickly.

"How about I go over everything with you?"

"I don't think that'll be necessary. You can send your final bill."

When he left, Summer felt as if she was going to faint while staring at the contents inside of that envelope. She watched how Honey and David slipped in and out of hotels and bars. In some photos they were holding hands, some kissing, just enjoying each other. She knew that this was after the shooting because David was walking with a cane that he required after the accident. Summer's whole body was on fire and her hands shook as she looked through the pictures.

She sat in the shop looking at the pictures and before she knew it an hour had passed. Revenge was on her mind. She was going to hire the best divorce lawyer his money could afford her and take him for everything he had. *What was she thinking? What was going on?* It was because of him that she decided to drop the charges against Honey for breaking the window. He told her they needed to let go of the past and going through a court case would be the equivalent of keeping that drama alive. Now she knew the real reason he wanted to drop them was because he didn't want his bitch in jail. She wouldn't be surprised if he bailed her out of jail when she was arrested. She made a mental note to check their bank statements for unexplainable withdrawals and then she would make a nice donation to herself.

...Constance

By the end of the week the story about Reggie and his mistress was the talk of the town. All the local news channels and newspapers picked up the story and all types of women began to come forward saying how they had also been between the sheets with the attorney. Reggie had gone into hiding, the anchorwoman resigned from her job and Patty; Reggie's wife had hired an attorney to set the divorce in motion. Constance couldn't help but feel a little guilty about the storm she created but also found it ironic that the one thing she wanted more than anything was making her feel guilty.

Summer asked her at least twice if she had any idea of how the tape got leaked to the media but she just denied knowing anything about it. This was a secret she was taking to her grave. Whenever someone on TV or radio would start talking about it she would change the channel. When she was in the shop there wasn't much she could do so she did her best to ignore it and hoped that the next scandal would knock this off the front pages.

It was a Saturday afternoon and the shop was packed. Monday was Labor Day and a lot of people that would be featured in the annual West Indian Day Parade were in the shop getting their weaves done. Constance was shocked that Summer was able to bounce back after kicking David out last week. That gesture took everyone by surprise. Even Constance knew for a fact that he was still seeing Honey. What was even more shocking was that she kicked David out last Saturday and was back at work on Monday. Summer was known for being emotional and dramatic about things like this. Constance figured she must've finally had enough of the bullshit.

Renee was in the shop today happier than she had been in a long time. She was so happy Sean was giving her another chance and she didn't know what to do with herself. Constance noticed a big change in her as well. This time around she was enjoying the love Sean was sending her way. Constance hadn't heard her speak of seeing another man since they got back together. One day last week she even witnessed her turn down a few men. She was proud of Renee because she knew it took a lot for someone like her to make such a drastic change.

"Ouch." Constance's customer said breaking her out of her daydream.

"Sorry but you need to keep still."

"You're braiding it too tight."

"Well keep still I'm almost finished."

Everything with Derrick was going great as he was turning out to be the man she had been looking for, for years. He knew his way around the kitchen as well as being able to do odd jobs around the house. He was great with her daughter and Meagan loved him. Even her mother was fond of him. Since they both worked long hours the time they spent together was valued and well spent. A lot of times if he got off work early he would pick Meagan up and they would come hang out at the shop until it was time for her to go. Until today the shop hadn't been too busy so Summer would let her leave early. She still had the $50,000 in the bank so she decided to put it in an account for her daughter. There wasn't much she needed or wanted in life right now that money could buy so she felt the money would be best not spent. As she finished her client's hair she smiled at herself knowing for the first time in her life she felt complete.

"That looks nice." Another client waiting to get her hair done said.

"Thank you."

"You should take a picture of that and submit it to a hair magazine."

"I already did. That's where she got it from."

"It really does look nice."

"Turn the volume up on the TV" Renee said "They're talking about Reggie again."

Constance rolled her eyes because she was getting sick of that story fast. She saw Summer watch the look that came across her face and knew what she was thinking. Constance could care less what people speculated, she would *never* admit to submitting that tape.

"Connie you should be happy your name wasn't mentioned in all of this."

Renee said.

"Why would my name be mentioned?"

"Connie I saw the tape and I recognized the room. I guess they only used her footage because she was famous and it caused a bigger scandal."

"Yeah I guess. I really don't care anymore."

"You knew him?" Mona asked sitting in Constance's chair to get her hair done.

"Barely." She lied.

"Barely." One of her regulars said. "Now girl you know you and that man was damn near in love with one another."

"Okay." Renee added.

"Well I'm not going to take this scandal and run with it like a lot of females I've seen coming out the woodwork talking about their relationship with him."

"I don't know why not, them chicks getting their 15 minutes of fame and probably a couple of dollars." Constance's client added

"Well I'll pass." Constance said not even looking at the latest episode of Reggies' scandal.

...Renee

Renee was shocked by Constance's ability to appear to not care about what was going on. She wasn't sure if it was because of her relationship with Derrick or something else. She knew first hand that Reggie getting a divorce was her biggest dream come true. Now that it was happening she was acting as if she could care less. Even if she had a negative reaction to all of the scandal it would've been some reaction but she acted as if she never knew the man.

Renee was in the shop today to get her nails done but she had also asked Summer to accompany her to the doctor this afternoon. She had asked her a week and a half ago so she hoped she didn't forget. Today was the day she was going to get her results from the doctor. She had taken an HIV test; something she had never done before and she was too afraid to get the results alone. Her doctor had told her the results were in days ago but she was scared to death to get them. She and Sean hadn't had sex since they got back together. She made a promise to God that if he spared her she would change her ways. As she watched Summer finish her clients' hair she wondered how her friend was really doing. From the outside she looked fine but Renee wondered how she was doing underneath that smile. Divorce was something Renee knew too well. Seeing the way her mother handled the whole ordeal made her sad for her friend.

"Renee I'll be ready to go once I'm done with her."

"Where are you going?" Constance asked.

"I promised her I would make a stop with her. I'll be back in a hour."

"Thanks Summer." She was thanking her for going, remembering and most importantly, not mentioning it to Constance.

She thought back to the night Sean was over and made a picnic for her in her living room. She couldn't remember once in their 4 years of being together ever talking like that. She enjoyed him so much and she was happy she was getting another chance at loving him. He made another "surprise" visit to her job the next day to meet her for lunch. This time he found her working and not getting worked over.

On the drive to the doctor's office she noticed that Summer's mind wasn't with them in the car. She sat in silence staring out the window. Renee decided to break it and tell Summer what was eating at her these past few weeks.

"Aren't you even curious as to why I asked you to escort me to the doctor?"

"I figured if you wanted me to know you would tell me."

"I took my first HIV test."

"Ever."

"Yes, ever. You sound surprised."

"Well I am a little surprised. I mean it's not like you're the Virgin Mary. I just figured you would've taken one. I'm married and I've taken one."

"Well this is my first and I'm scared to death."

"You have nothing to be scared of. You'll be fine."

"Terrence put his hands on me." There she said it, finally.

"What!" Summer exclaimed now giving Renee all of her attention. "When?"

"A few weeks ago, it's over now."

"Why didn't you say anything? Have you mentioned this to Frog?"

"No, of course not, I did call him that night but I didn't say anything about what happened. I don't want anybody outside of this car to know about this."

"Okay."

"I have a secret of my own."

"You?"

"Yes me."

"What's up?"

"A week before I found out David was still seeing Honey we were finally starting to turn our marriage around. We even started having sex again. So I was beyond shocked to learn that he was still having sex with Honey." Renee looked at her wondering what she meant when she said "they started having sex again." No wonder she wasn't getting pregnant, she wasn't even having sex. Instead of speaking she just listened.

"It's because of him that I dropped the charges against Honey. I feel so stupid."

"Don't beat up on yourself for loving your husband. He was the ass who couldn't appreciate all that you were willing to give him."

"I know, but that's not even the worst of it."

"There's more."

"The night that I approached him about everything he told me that Honey was pregnant by him."

Renee just stared at her in disbelief as she listened to her friend finally open up and get her problems off her chest.

...Summer

On her way home from the shop after the investigator's visit she was fuming. She was feeling a rage she had never experienced before. She felt betrayed, lied to, cheated on and most of all played for a fool. How could she be so blind as to not see the signs...again? When she pulled into her driveway it was after 10 and surprisingly David's car was there. She gathered her things and walked into the house.

When she entered the house she was met with the aroma of food. The kitchen table was set for two and there was an envelope on the table with her name on it. She opened it up and read the instructions telling her to meet him upstairs in the in the master bathroom. As she ripped the note and threw it in the trash she made her way upstairs past the empty living room. After he came home from the hospital they had cleaned the room and discarded all of the damaged furniture.

As she entered her bedroom she looked over the pictures of their wedding day. What was the happiest day of her life had crumbled to a distant memory. When she entered the bathroom he was in the bubble bath sipping on a glass of wine.

"Welcome home beautiful." He said a bit tipsy. She just stood at the door tears blurring her eye sight. Tomorrow she would be contacting a divorce lawyer to finally end this charade.

"Come join me, baby." He said handing her a glass. She took it and sat on the toilet seat next to the tub. He handed her the wine as he sipped on his. "So how was your day?" He asked as he grabbed her hand and kissed it. She had once genuinely loved this man. Now she was on the verge of telling him that the love was no longer there. She had to tell this man she wanted a divorce. She sat and stared at him as he kissed and sucked on her fingers. She pulled her hand away sharply.

"I'm here to get a change of clothes. I'm going to stay in a hotel tonight so I can give you time to get all of your shit. When I get home tomorrow I want you out."

David sat upright in the tub.

"What are you talking about? What's the matter?"

"Do not sit there and look at me like you have no idea what I could possibly be talking about. And I don't want to hear no more of your bullshit excuses because I've heard enough of them to last me a lifetime."

"Summer, what is the problem? Talk to me."

"There is no need to explain something you already know. The only thing you need to know is that I know. I want you out of my house by the time I get back." She stood up and went into the bedroom to gather a few things for the night. As she packed David jumped out of the tub and was in the room on her tail naked, dripping wet with bubbles.

"Summer if this has anything to do with Honey I swear I just ended it with her."

How dare he stand in her face, in her bedroom and tell her he *just* ended it with her. Without responding she continued to gather her things.

"Did she contact you Summer? You can't believe anything she says. She's just upset that I ended it with her. Can't you see that?"

As she watched her husband plead she almost felt sorry for him.

"David I don't want to hear it anymore."

He grabbed her by her hand to stop her from walking away from him.

"Summer, I need you right now." She snatched her hand back from him.

"*You* need *me* David? Where were you when I needed you? After everything we went through with this bitch you had the nerve, the audacity to go back to her. You protected that bitch this whole time. You had the gall to talk me into dropping charges against her. For what! So you could continue to fuck her! Don't you dare stand here and tell me you need me."

"No matter what happens between us, I want you to know that I love you. Between the pressure with work and us trying to make this marriage work, I guess I lost myself. I know I can't make excuses for this but it's the truth."

"You've been working since I met you and we've been trying to get pregnant forever, so why all of a sudden is everything so stressful?" She was not trying to hear any of his excuses and pleas tonight.

"I've done things that I shouldn't but..." His voice trailed off as he searched for the right words. "Do you know how hard this has been on me?" He sat on the bed with his shoulders slouched before he continued. "She told me she was pregnant."

Summer heard him but the slap that she put across his face resonated louder than his words. Her whole body felt numb as her legs weakened and she felt as if she was on the verge of passing out. She wanted to scream but nothing would come out.

"Pumpkin, please understand that's the only reason I needed you to drop the charges. If I couldn't talk her into getting an abortion I couldn't see her pregnant in jail with my child." She slapped him again. He was so torn emotionally that her successive slaps had no impact.

"Don't call me Pumpkin motherfucker. You were fucking that whore raw?" She couldn't believe in addition to cheating.... Again... he had put her at such a great risk. She was through.

"Don't be ridiculous. I would never do something like that. Guess she took the condom out of the garbage and inserted the sperm." He said with a straight face.

"You expect me to stand here and say what? I can't tell you how much I hate you right now. I'm done with your sorry ass." She said continuing to pack her bags. She wanted to get the fuck away from him faster than she could say the word divorce.

"I only kept seeing her because I was trying to talk her into getting rid of it. You really think I want a baby with her?"

"David that is no longer my problem or concern. When I get home tomorrow I want you out. I suggest you take anything of value with you because I'm changing the locks and you're not getting anything until after the divorce is final and everything's been divvied up.

"Divorce! Are you losing your mind? You can go stay with Constance for a few days to calm down if you want but you must be crazy if you think you're leaving me." He said grabbing at her hands which she snatched away before he could reach it.

"Don't you dare touch me you nasty motherfucker! Stop it! And you need to know that I ain't crazy no more. Yesterday and maybe even today but right now at this very moment you had better believe that I stand here a sane woman." She said as she stood up, grabbed her bag and left. On her way down the stairs she started an uncontrollable laugh as she knocked down pictures of happier times off the wall. She decided to check into a hotel and try to enjoy herself and relax. She headed to the city because she planned to check into a nice high priced hotel for the night. She would try and get a day of beauty tomorrow. She felt she was well over due at caring for Summer and from this point on that was the first person she planned to treat better.

...Renee

As Summer and Renee left the doctors office, Renee was on cloud nine. She was so happy that her results were negative she was now free to love Sean both emotionally and physically. They had talked on the phone last night for almost 3 hours. Absence certainly did make the heart grow fonder.

Once she dropped Summer back off at the shop she had the urge to go shopping. She had taken the day off from work because of her doctor's appointment. She felt like celebrating and the best way to do that was to shop. And she knew just where she was headed, Victoria's Secret. She had planned to buy a sexy outfit, go home and shower and show up to his job and give him one as well.

When she arrived at the mall she ended up making a few in between stops before she actually made it into Victoria's Secret. When she entered the store she had shopping bags in both hands and struggled past a young couple giggling on their way out. As she searched through the items the sales woman came and asked her if she needed any help. She turned to say no when she realized the woman asking was Sean's current flame Tracy.

"Well Hello."

A look of disappointment came across Tracy's face once she saw the customer needing help was Renee.

"Look, I'll find someone else to help you."

"No need. I already have what I want." She said obviously referring to Sean.

"Well good for you." Tracy said with a fake smile. "I hope you're happy with your selection."

"Extremely, and I guess I'm not so tacky after all huh?"

"What?" Tracy said with an attitude.

"You heard me. In Sean's office you said me still wearing my ring was tacky."

"I don't care about you or your ring. Frog and I are over because I don't deal with men who are unfaithful. But whatever makes you happy. Now if you'll excuse me I'm at work." Tracy walked away leaving Renee standing there holding the garment that would seal the deal of them getting back together. She was happy to hear it from both horses' mouths that they were over. She just automatically assumed that she was the girl Tracy referred to as him being unfaithful with.

...Constance

As Constance laid in her bed watching the ceiling fan spin she was contemplating going to the parade. Her daughter really wanted to go and had even dressed up in clothing that incorporated the Jamaican flag. She came to the conclusion that she'd ask Derrick if he could take Meagan without her. Not only did she not feel festive she didn't want to take the chance of running into Reggie. She figured despite the recent scandal he would be on the radio's float again this year, trying to keep up a good face. As her daughter and Derrick came in the room she could see the disappointment on their faces when they saw she still wasn't dressed.

"Mom why aren't you dressed yet?"

"Baby, Mommy doesn't feel like going."

"Please mom." Meagan begged.

"You feeling all right?" Derrick asked feeling her forehead.

"Yeah I'm fine, just tired. You guys should still go. Don't let me spoil your fun."

"You sure? We could rent some movies or just watch the parade on TV." Derrick said as he sat down on the bed next to her ever accommodating.

"No, I want to go. You promised that I could go." Meagan whined.

"Go. I want you guys to go. I'll be here looking for you on TV." She said giving Derrick a reassuring look that everything was okay. "Come on I'll walk you to the car." She said getting up slipping on a pair of jeans and a top. She grabbed her bag and keys and headed out. All she wanted to do was grab something to eat, go upstairs and get back in her bed. As she watched them drive off she smiled thinking what a good man Derrick was. He was the first person to come in their lives and not only care so much about her but also about her daughter.

After getting some food from the local West Indian restaurant she headed back upstairs to enjoy some time to herself. Since she started dating Derrick she couldn't remember the last time she had some "alone" time. As she got off the elevator she laughed to herself thinking how she couldn't believe she looked forward to enjoying "alone" time.

As she stepped off the elevator, while digging in her bag looking for her keys, she heard the stairway door open and turned to see the large silhouette of a man step out. The man had on a pair of raggedy jeans and a tee shirt. The baseball cap he wore was low and he looked haggard as if he needed a shave. The closer he got the more recognizable he became. She stood frozen as she saw Reggie quickly walking towards her with an object that resembled a gun tucked in his waistband.

"Aren't you going to say hello?" He asked as he pushed her against the wall grinding himself against her as he whispered. "Open the door and don't try anything stupid or Meagan's coming home to find her mother laid out in the hallway."

As she felt the nuzzle of the gun pressed against her abdomen her heart froze, then raced uncontrollably.

She wanted to move but she couldn't. Her mind was racing in so many directions at once she couldn't think straight. The nudge he gave her let her know she needed to open the door as well as anything else he ordered her to do. Once they were in the apartment he ordered her to sit in the kitchen chair. As he pointed the gun at her she noticed how steady his hand was. Here was the most dangerous of creatures; a man that had lost everything and had nothing else to lose. Constance on the other hand had everything to lose. She needed to do something and fast. As her mind started to catch up with her body she wanted to kick herself for opening the door. Now she had to figure out a way to get this fool out of her apartment.

"Reggie what's going on?" She asked trying not to let the fear be heard in her voice.

"Don't fucking question me!" As he began to speak she could smell the strong scent of alcohol on his breath. "You know exactly why I'm here. Now where the fuck is the tape?"

"Reggie, I don't know..."

"..Don't even try it! I asked you once not to fuck with me!" He yelled.

At that moment Constance feared Reggie like she had never feared anyone before. She wasn't sure to what extent he would go to recover the tape, but she was willing to do anything to save her life.

"Reggie, are you gonna shoot me?"

Reggie slapped her across her face. The force of the slap was so hard she flew from the chair to the floor. As her body hit the ground her keys and bag went flying with her. She laid there holding the side of her face. She couldn't believe he just slapped her. She hadn't been hit since Meagan's father. Reggie knew more than anyone how she felt about that as she had shared this with him on several occasions.

With all the strength she had in her she responded by grabbing her overstuffed Coach bag and swung for his head. Anything that was left in the bag from her fall went flying everywhere. He blocked the blow with his right hand and came up and caught her square to the jaw with his left. This time when she hit the floor he made sure she wasn't getting up to swing anything. She laid there and watched him as he started searching through her apartment, muttering to himself while cursing. An acute pain shot from her head as blood poured slowly from her mouth. She was sure her jaw was broken.

"Did you really think I wasn't going to find out you gave the fucking media that tape? I still got connections. Didn't you think if somebody paid your dumb ass to tell a story I could pay somebody to tell yours? But of course it didn't take no genius to figure out it was you. You were the last person I had in there before my shit came up missing. I thought it was one of the maids snooping around but then it dawned on me that I haven't heard from you since that night. What a fucking coincidence. And what happens? I come back to see you done caught jungle fever on a nigga."

She couldn't respond because of the pain in her mouth. While he stumbled drunkenly through the house searching for the tape she spotted her camera that she kept in her purse; ironically in an effort to catch Reggie's wife messing around. She grabbed it quickly and without turning on the flash took numerous shots of him as he walked from room to room. She also took a picture of herself so that whoever found the camera would know exactly who did this to her. When she heard him on his way out of the room she flung the camera under the sofa.

As she saw him approaching her with the gun pointed to her head she said a silent prayer to God and hoped that he was listening.

...Summer

For the past few days that David was gone Summer had felt so free. Over the years she had devoted so much time and effort into making her marriage work that she became buried in it. Now that she was in the process of getting a divorce she felt liberated. The happiness that she hoped to find through having a baby was actually realized by knowing she was starting the divorce process. She would've never guessed that a divorce would bring so much calmness and easiness to her life.

When she reached home the day after she kicked David out she was relieved that he took her threat seriously and was now gone. She contacted a locksmith and called a few divorce lawyers and the like. She planned to get a few things done around the house. The shop wouldn't be open today because of Labor Day so she could devote her time to her personal business. Despite the freedom afforded by her estrangement from David, she knew once she started putting his things away she just might break down from the emotion. She called Constance all afternoon to ask her to come over and help but her machine kept picking up. Summer figured she must've decided to go to the parade after all. Renee was spending the day with Sean at his parent's house upstate. This was the first time he had ever invited her up to his parent's house. The few times she did meet them they had always come to visit.

Summer decided she would start in the bedroom. She figured if she could get through that room successfully she could do the rest of the house with no problem. She was still young and needed to live more. She decided that when everything was done and over with she would buy a condo. During her marriage it was always more work and less fun. Because she accomplished what she set out to do as far as her business she was now ready to have some fun. With the money she would get from selling the house she planned to expand and redo the shop just the way she wanted. It was her time.

Yes, Summer thought to herself as she headed up the stairs ready to pack up her past and make way for her future. It was her time.

...Renee

As soon as they pulled up to his parents house Renee saw a side of Sean she hadn't seen before. The big brick house with the two car garage was where Sean grew up. He rarely spoke of his childhood or his family. Whenever Renee would talk about her family he would listen and console her if needed. But he hardly ever spoke of his past. She knew he grew up upstate in Monticello as an only child and that he spent his summers in Queens at his grandmother's house.

They had decided to come, spend the weekend and stay for his family's annual BBQ.

"Are you nervous?" He asked as he rung the bell.

"No not really."

"You should be." He said before he smiled.

His mother opened the door and the look on her face would've never told what she was thinking.

"Sean dear how are you?" She said as she kissed his cheek.

"I'm fine." He replied as they followed her inside.

"Hello Renee, it's nice to see you again."

"You too."

"I had no idea you were coming. Why didn't you tell me she was coming with you Sean? I'll have to set an extra place for dinner." She said as she headed off to the kitchen.

"Where's Daddy?" He asked as he took the bags from Renee and headed up to his old room.

"He went to the store and should be on his way back now." His mother said heading into the kitchen.

"Let me show you where you'll be sleeping."

"We aren't sleeping together?"

"I'll see what I can work out." He said smiling. When she entered his old room she was impressed with the awards that adorned the walls. He had a few family pictures throughout the room. She quietly watched him as he headed towards the night stand and stared at a picture of him and his grandmother. She walked over to him and hugged him from behind.

"You alright?"

"Yeah." He said turning towards her to give her a hug. "Love you."

She hadn't heard him say that to her in so long. She wished she could savor this moment forever. "I love you too." And she buried her head in his chest inhaling him until his mother called him from downstairs.

"Come on." He said taking her by the hands leading her downstairs.

When they reached the landing Sean's father was just coming into the house. Sean strongly resembled his father. He gave his father a hug before taking the grocery bags and heading to the kitchen.

"Hey Renee I didn't know you were coming up." He said giving her a kiss on the cheek.

"Yeah, it was decided at the last minute."

When they joined his mother in the kitchen there were two women who sat on one side of the table talking and drinking tea with her. The elder of the two women looked like an older version of the young woman sitting next to her. Renee assumed they must be mother and daughter but she didn't remember him ever mentioning any female cousins growing up.

"Charles." Mrs. Billings called out to her husband as they entered the kitchen. "Can you help me out in the garage? I forgot to bring the sodas in from the refrigerator."

"Charlotte, I just got in from the store and you already trying to put me back to work." He playfully replied following her out the door.

There was an awkward moment until the elder of the two women spoke.

"Have you lost your manners Sean?" She asked him with a hint of rudeness in her voice.

"No, of course I haven't. How are you this afternoon Mrs. Brown? Felicia?" He asked as he pulled out a seat next to him for Renee and sat down himself.

"I'm fine." The mother replied.

"That's good."

"Aren't you going to introduce us to your friend?" The younger one said with jealousy in her eyes that Renee noticed right away. She stood about 5'9 and weighed no more than 130 lbs. Her hair was pulled up and twisted in a hair clip. She wore little make up and didn't need much to bring out her beautiful features.

"I will if you give me a chance. Renee, this is Felicia and her mother Fancy."

She made sure to shake Felicia's hand with her left.

"It's nice to meet you." Felicia said smiling.

Renee could sense her presence wasn't too welcomed. Especially by the mother who couldn't hide signs from her face and body expressions. She sat at the table with her chin in her hand staring at the two of them.

"So what brings you two out this early? I didn't expect to see you till the BBQ on Monday."

"Well your mom told my mom that you were here visiting so I stopped by to say hello. And she invited us to stay for dinner."

Oh really

"Okay." He said grabbing an apple out the fruit bowl on the table.

"Is that an engagement ring on your finger?" Fancy, Felicia's mother asked almost afraid of the answer.

"Yes." Renee said she seemed to be the only one smiling. The situation was getting uncomfortable.

"Really?" Felicia said in an unbelievable laugh.

"Yep I'm getting married." Sean answered.

"To her?" Fancy said rudely.

"Yes to her." Sean said grabbing Renee's hand under the table indicating that she should let him handle this.

"Well congratulations to both of you." Felicia said putting on her best fake smile that wasn't doing a good job of hiding her pain.

"Thank you." Sean said.

"Are you guy's hungry?" Mrs. Billings asked as she started to place dinner on the dining room table. Sean's father walked in behind her and took a seat at the table. "So how's everybody doing this afternoon?" He said smiling.

"So when's the big day?" Felicia asked probing, ignoring his question.

"Sometime next July." Renee answered tired of sitting mute between what ever what was going on between them.

"Sean you make sure I get my invitation."

Invitation?

"I'm sorry but I'm confused by your relationship to Sean. Are you his cousin, god sister?" Renee asked ready to get to the bottom of all of this.

"Felicia and I dated off and on over the years."

"Dated? I think we did a little more than date Sean."

"Could we please talk about this after we eat?" Sean's mother asked making her plate.

"Yeah when I was 25 that was like 8 years ago I was young so I call it dating."

"If you say so Sean, we'll just leave it at that."

"Weren't you two just together?" Fancy added

"Mother I said leave it." She said forcing that fake smile for the remainder of the evening which was spent awkwardly quiet. They made small talk about what was going on in the local news. Renee smiled on the outside but she was fuming on the inside.

When she finally got a chance alone later that night she questioned him to try and get a better understanding of what was going on.

"What was that all about?" Renee asked. His parents were in the room watching TV, Felicia and her mother went home and her and Sean were putting the dishes in the dishwasher.

"What?" he answered innocently.

"You know what. Did you sleep with her?"

"Renee we dated for two years of course I slept with her."

"You know what I'm talking about and your smart ass answers aren't helping your case."

"I didn't know I was on trial." Sean replied in a more serious tone.

"When was the last time you slept with her?"

"What! I'm not answering that"

"I knew it. She basically said it and there is no way she would be that bitter if you hadn't just slept with her."

"Look, I don't have to explain myself to you about a relationship that's over. Even if I did sleep with her recently we weren't together."

"That's the point. You bring me up here without telling anyone, knowing it was a possibility that *she* could've been here. Then you have me sit here and break bread with somebody you broke a piece off in."

"Look I'm not going to fight with you over something that's nothing. I didn't know she was going to be here today and that's the last I'm talking to you about this."

Renee knew that pushing him wasn't going to get her anything but more frustrated. After all they had been through within the past few months she wasn't trying to go backwards. She knew she wasn't innocent during the time they were apart so she couldn't fault him for what he did. Not to mention the fact that tonight he made it known who was important in his life so she happily let it go.

...Summer

Listening to her Sade CD as she cleaned out David's closet put Summer in a strange and unbalanced mood. She felt like a snake in the process of shedding its skin. Summer was thinking of all the changes that would be taking place in her life shortly. She planned to go back to school to get her masters degree and maybe open up another shop in Harlem. She had been reading about Harlem's resurgence for sometime now and she wanted a piece of that cake. "You gave me the kiss of life, kiss of life. Oh yeah, oh yeah." She sang as she folded his sweaters and coats into a box. The ringing of the phone broke her optimistic thoughts.

"Hello."

"Summer. It's Derrick can you get over to Connie's and pick up Meagan?"

"Why, where's Connie?"

"Summer, just get over here, now." He hung up before she could say anything else. She didn't like the tone in his voice and why did she all of a sudden have to pick up Meagan? Summer told herself not to think the worst and to just get over there and see what was going on. She threw on a pair of jeans and sneakers grabbed her car keys and headed out.

As Summer approached Constance's block her heart got lost in her chest. There were red and blue lights flashing everywhere. The fire department and a few cop cars were pulled up in front of her building. There were a few news vans and cops were literally everywhere. Some were questioning people, some were holding spectators back, while others looked around for evidence. She felt as if she was going to faint when one of Connie's neighbors came over to her crying uncontrollably. The woman she recognized was Tammy, who would leave her kids over Connie's from time to time to play with Meagan. Tammy hugged Summer and kept repeating how sorry she was and that she couldn't believe something like this could happen. Once Summer was able to calm her down she asked.

"Tammy, what happened?"

"I saw her Summer. I was on my way downstairs when I heard Derrick scream…I just ran inside. She was lying in a pool of blood, I mean blood was everywhere. He kept yelling for me to call 911 but I was in shock. Who in the hell would do something like this to her?" Tammy started crying again as a lump so large formed in Summer's throat that she couldn't swallow it. As Summer made her way through the crowd she tried to convince herself that Tammy didn't know what she was talking about.

She made it to the building where cops were preventing people from going in and coming out.

"Excuse me officer my name is Summer Johnson and I think something happened to my sister?" Summer said her voice cracking.

"What's your sister's name?" The officer asked.

"Constance Simmons." He called out to another cop who directed Summer to a squad car where she saw Derrick and Meagan sitting inside. Meagan was asleep while Derrick sat there with his head in his hands sobbing. Summer later learned that this was the last image she saw before she lost consciousness.

...Renee

On the final day of the trip Renee was glad she would be returning home soon. As much as she enjoyed spending time at his parent's house she missed sleeping in her own bed. She couldn't believe she had slept so late today. She didn't want to come across as a bad house guest. When she got up she realized that Sean got up and left her sleeping till after two o'clock in the afternoon. After she dressed she headed downstairs to smell of BBQ in the air. It was going on 4 o'clock and guests had already begun to arrive. Felicia and her mother Fancy, were out back having salad and chicken talking to Sean and his mother. His father was on the grill talking to a couple of men who stood around him drinking beer. Two of Sean's aunts that Renee had met the previous day sat at the table sipping wine.

"Hey baby." Sean said as he walked over and greeted her.

"Hey, why didn't you wake me?" she whispered in his ear as he kissed her on the cheek.

"I tried but you were knocked out so I figured I might as well let you rest."

"Still, you shouldn't have let me sleep so late. I see the party's already starting."

"Yeah everybody knows if you wanna eat you better get here before now. I put a plate aside for you if you're hungry."

"No I'm good."

The rest of the night went off without a hitch. So when Sean asked her if they could stay till morning she had no problem when she said "yes."

It was the end of the night. Sean and Renee were snuggled up on his parents couch like high schoolers watching TV when his phone rang. He didn't say much after hello or after he hung up. She noticed immediately the change in his demeanor and wondered what could be wrong.

"What happened?" Renee asked, but he ignored her question. He sat in silence staring at the TV but not staring at the TV. He finally turned the television off and turned to her with tears in his eyes.

"Baby what happened?"

"That was Derrick."

"Okay."

"Somebody killed Constance. He said he wanted to tell me before I heard it on the news."

"Who?" Even though Renee heard him say Constance she knew it couldn't be.

"Constance, baby."

"What?" *What is going on? Constance murdered?*

"Are you okay?" He asked seeing that she was in a state of shock.

"We gotta go home." She said getting up.

"Renee wait." He said grabbing her hand. "It's late. We should wait till morning when our heads are clear and its some light out."

She stood and looked at him as the tears that formed in her eyes made their way down her cheek to the corner of her mouth.

"One of my best friends was just murdered. I don't care what time of the night it is. I'm leaving. If you want to stay then stay. Summer's alone. Constance is dead. Oh God why?" She cried as he held her in his arms.

"We'll leave now. I'm sorry. I'll go and pack our stuff and tell my parents that we're leaving."

He headed upstairs while Renee called Summer.

...Summer

When Summer woke up in the hospital she had an I.V in her arm and her throat was dry. A nurse was checking her pulse smiling at her like she knew her.

"Hey baby it's nice to see you awake." She said with a thick Jamaican accent.

Summer looked at her trying to remember what happened. Before she could ask the question David appeared behind the nurse smiling. *What is going on?*

"Hey how you feeling?" He asked with red eyes. She could tell he was crying and that's when she remembered Constance's neighbor crying telling her what she saw. An uneasy pain stirred in her heart as she tried to come to terms with what was happening. She looked at David for an answer and he gave her a hug as she came to grips with everything that happened.

When Summer reached home she was drained mentally and physically. After being released from the hospital later that evening she went to Constance's mother's house. Her whole family was grieving, while a few news reporters were still lingering around outside the house trying to get some type of information or interview. David had assisted her and was her rock in this time of need. At the end of the night he had wanted to come inside and at first she declined his offer. She was not going to use Constance's death as a reason to do something she would regret later.

As soon as she walked into her living room she felt it. Alone. She had no one, no baby, mother, husband and now her sister was gone. She sat on the floor by the door crying until David got there and put her to bed. When she woke up the next morning to the ringing phone her head was killing her.

"Hello." She answered trying to focus her eyes. She felt as if she had a hangover. The person on the other line was crying and she realized right away that she hadn't called Renee.

"Renee?"

"Why didn't you call me? I've been trying to call you all night." Renee cried into the phone.

"I'm so sorry. Everything has just been happening so fast." Summer apologized.

"Are you going to be home?" Renee asked.

"Um yeah, yeah I'll be here." Summer said as she looked over at her clothes on the floor. *Where is David?*

"Sean and I are on our way over right now." She said hanging up.

      Summer got out of bed and went to see if David was downstairs but he was gone. She was a little relieved that he wasn't there because she wasn't sure how she would deal with him. What happened last night was a combination of the moment and the emotion derived from it. She was not about to change her mind about the divorce and start over. She decided to jump in the shower and get dressed before Frog and Renee arrived.

...Renee

Renee sat hanging onto Summer's every word as she told her what she could remember about everything that happened. She explained the way Tammy described what she saw at Constance's apartment that day. Renee's heart went out to Summer and Constances' family. Even though they got into it sometime she did love Constance very much.

"How's Meagan holding up?"

"She's doing fine from what Carmen told me. Considering." Summer said dabbing the tissue in her hand to her eyes.

"I still can't believe this happened. I feel like it's surreal, you know? Who would do something like that to her? Come into her house and murder her like that." Renee said getting a headache from all that was happening.

"I don't know. The cops asked me if I knew of anyone who would want to hurt her. And I couldn't think of a single person."

"What about Honey?"

"I don't think she's capable of doing something like that."

"Why not? She could've gotten one of those guys down at the club to do it for her."

"You watch too much of that First 48 nonsense."

"Then who Summer? It's like you said, there isn't a single person you could think of." Renee said confused.

...Summer

Opening the shop was a hard thing to do without Constance around. Summer was grateful that Renee had taken time off of work to help her around the shop while she tried to get through the madness. She waited almost a month after the murder before she opened the shop back up. Customers came in and supported the shop in a way that she couldn't imagine. People brought money, food, flowers, plants, pictures that they had taken with Constance at gatherings or after she did a style for them. An artist came by and spray painted a mural on the gate of the shop. Summer hired a fill in to come in and help around the shop as Renee had no intention of washing anybody's hair. Even though a lot of things had changed some things remained the same.

Today was Sunday and the shop was closed. She was on her way to drop Meagan off at her grandmother's house. Since the funeral, Constance's mother grew to rely on Summer to help out with Meagan. Meagan was taking everything quite well, and aside from a few occasional breakdowns, she was holding it together. She had returned to school and was also seeing a therapist to talk about anything she wanted. Summer knew it must've been hard to find out that a man she knew had taken her mother's life. It was hard for Summer to look at the girl and not cry, since she so strongly resembled her mother.

Summer's phone started to ring but she didn't answer it because she knew it was Renee asking where she was. She was running a little late this afternoon because she and Meagan had went and did a little shopping after leaving the house. She was supposed to meet Renee a half hour ago to help her look at Wedding dresses. She was happy that Renee and Frog was able to work through their differences. She was also envious of their love and only hoped she could find a man who could love her through just about anything. Frog had the patience and maturity to realize Renee had made a mistake and was willing to do anything to make it up to him. Whereas with her husband when she tried to love him through his mistake, he just threw it back in her face. She was willing to forgive him for cheating up until the point that he got caught but when he went back to Honey after being caught she knew she had to let him go.

Had Summer been paying closer attention to her surroundings, she would've saw her husband walking hurriedly into a known spot as she drove past. Had she paid closer attention to her surroundings and focused less on her getting pregnant she would've saw that Honey wasn't her husband's only addiction.

...David

David recently was served the divorce papers signaling the end of his marriage. As a result he dove deeper and deeper into his habit. He still stayed with Honey, but she was even growing sick of him. They went out less and less while he indulged more and more. He became paranoid, often telling her that people were following him. She was about to kick him out until his words proved correct. One morning after returning home from work she came up on two men assaulting David in front of her building. She had given them all of her tip money for the night which came close to $600.00 to make them leave him alone. Before departing she heard one of the men tell David if he didn't have the rest of the money by the end of the month they'd be back. In addition to his debts, he now had to worry about hearing Honey's mouth about putting her at risk by letting drug enforcers know where she lived. Things had quickly turned for the worse for David.

"You still haven't found a place for us to stay David?" She asked walking around in her panties and bra, picking up clothes that were scattered throughout the house.

"Don't worry. If worse comes to worse we'll stay in a hotel. But I doubt they'll be back." He said laying on the couch trying to watch the game on TV.

"Oh really? And what makes you think that smart ass? Did you pay them their money?"

"No, not all of it."

"That's what the fuck I thought. So what makes you think they won't come back?"

"Well, it's been over a month and you haven't seen them, have you?"

"What the fuck does that mean David? You know what, it's your life, you just better make sure I don't get caught up in your shit. Because next time I'm a let them kill your ass." She said as she stormed off to her room. David was getting fed up with her and her big mouth. He couldn't help but kick himself in the ass for all the trouble he brought on himself and the people around him. But it was too late to turn back time.

He made the age old addict's mistake of getting high on credit in an effort to hide his habit from his wife. He knew if she saw significant amounts of money missing from the account she would immediately question him. So he tried to pay a little here and a little there but as it always does, it all caught up to him after awhile. He was now in debt for close to $50,000 because of his dying devotion to the drug. After Summer kicked him out she damn near cleaned out their joint bank account and since the house wasn't up for sale yet he had no way of getting his hands on that type of money anytime soon. He thought he was in the clear when Reggie approached him almost two months ago trying to get information about who could've leaked that tape to the press. Since he was in the television/ radio advertising industry he had connections and could easily find out that information. And for the money Reggie was offering it was a no brainer. For $25,000 all he had to do was give a name. Once he found out it was Connie's name he felt even better about what he was doing. It was time that her big ass mouth paid the piper. Much to his surprise Reggie snapped and killed Constance. And even worse getting caught and arrested before he could give David a dime.

Now he laid on his whore's couch listening to her bitch and moan about shit he had no control over. He knew she was right, just because they didn't come back 30 days later did not mean they weren't coming.

He learned that lesson the night they came to his house and shot him. At the time he was in the hole for $20k and had so many open ended promises that he finally decided he would put up his custom furniture as collateral to buy him some more time. Much to his surprise, when he got home that night the furniture had been destroyed by his wife, taking any value that it had with it. He couldn't believe the timing of the shit. If it wasn't for bad luck he'd have no luck at all.

"David! I'm getting sick and tired of living in fear, you need to make this shit right now!"

"Honey please, I'm getting sick and tired of hearing your fucking Mouth!"

"Then do what you gotta do."

"Man, fuck this." David got up, put on some clothes and left. He ended up going to a local after hour coke spot where he had been frequenting for the past few weeks to get high.

David was so into what he was doing that he didn't see or hear the two large men come up to him until one of them hit him in the back of his head with the butt of the gun. As he lay on the floor holding his head the other man kicked him in his stomach.

"Where's Joe's money?"

The pain in his head coupled with the fact that he didn't have the money prevented him from answering.

"I said… where-the-fuck-is-Joe's-money?" The man yelled, annunciating each word as he kicked him repeatedly. The other addicts in the spot scattered once they saw the attempted collection taking place. They silently thanked God that they weren't on the receiving end.

"Please don't hit me again. I'll have the money by the end of the week."

"You had over a month to get that paper together. Joe's tired of waiting and he's out of messages to be sent to you."

"Please don't kill me."

"You're already dead." The man said as he put the gun in David's mouth and pulled the trigger.

...*Constance*

Constance was gone but never forgotten. She was there when Renee and Frog finally said their I do's. She watched Summer fall in love all over again. She smiled when she saw her daughter shop for her first prom dress with Renee and Summer.

Just as she watched David plead for his life before he was sent to meet his maker. But as she watched Reggie get shipped on the bus upstate to serve his 25 to life prison term. It wasn't him who she watched. It was the man that waited in the shadows watching him. It was Meagan's father Matthew.